Table of Contents

©2003 by Evan-Moor Corp. • Basic Math Skills, Grade 1 • EMC 3014

Introduction

Basic Math Skills is based on current NCTM standards and is designed to support any math curriculum that you may be using in your classroom. The standard strands (Number and Operations, Algebra, Geometry, Measurement, and Data Analysis and Probability) and skills within the strand are listed on the overview page for each section of the book. The skill is also shown at the bottom of each reproducible page.

Opportunities to practice the process standards (Problem Solving, Reasoning and Proof, Communications, Connections, and Representations) are also provided as students complete the various types of activities in this resource book.

Basic Math Skills may be used as a resource providing practice of skills already introduced to students. Any page may be used with an individual child, as homework, with a small group, or by the whole class.

Skill Practice

Each skill is covered in a set of six reproducible pages that include the following:

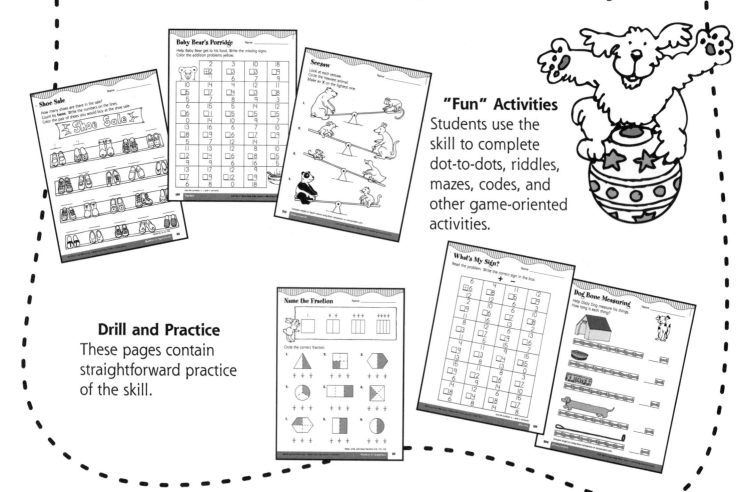

"Fun" Activities
Students use the skill to complete dot-to-dots, riddles, mazes, codes, and other game-oriented activities.

Drill and Practice
These pages contain straightforward practice of the skill.

EMC 3014 • Basic Math Skills, Grade 1 • ©2003 by Evan-Moor Corp.

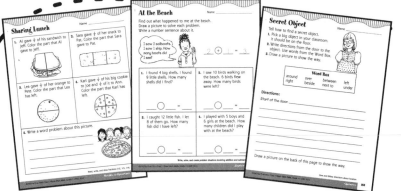

Application/Word Problem Activities

Students use the skill to problem solve and explore real-life situations.

Math Test

A test in standardized format is provided for each skill.

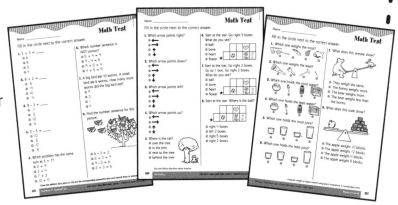

Additional Resources

The following additional resources are also provided:

- Timed math tests
- Class record sheet
- Test answer form
- Awards
- Reproducible practice cards for addition and subtraction facts

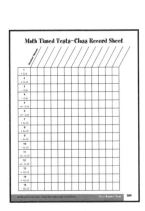

Number and Operations

On Your Mark, Get Set, Go!

Name _____

Color the numbers in order from **1** to **20** to find your way to the finish line.

 Start

1	2	3	7	9	11	4
6	8	4	5	0	2	8
8	11	12	6	10	7	13
15	9	8	7	12	16	5
14	10	17	11	17	18	19
6	11	12	9	16	10	20
20	18	13	14	15	Finish	

Count, read, and write whole numbers to 20

Number & Operations

Who Is It?

Start at **1**.
Connect the dots.

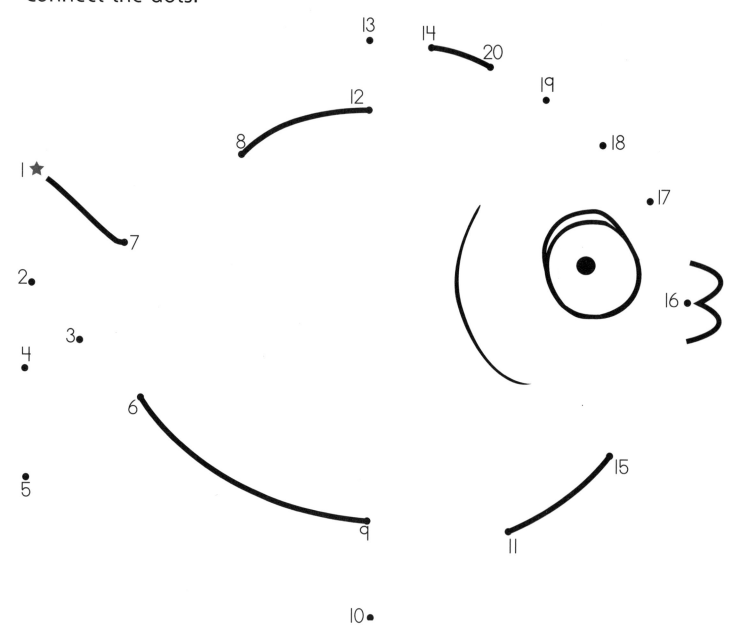

Mark the fish you made.

  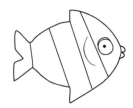

Count, read, and write whole numbers to 20

Count to 20

Name _____

Write the missing numbers.

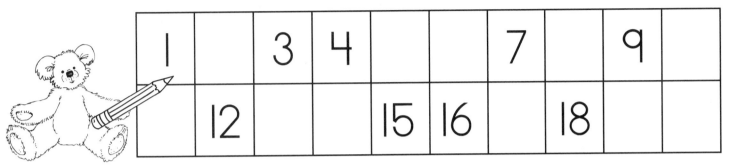

1		3	4			7		9	
	12			15	16			18	

Write the numbers **1** to **20**.

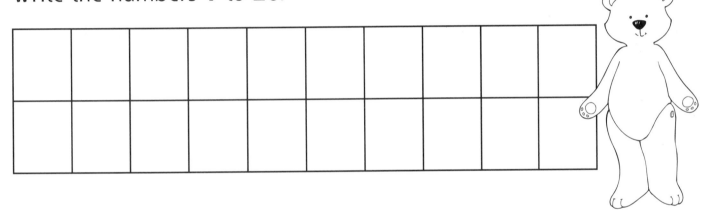

Circle **20** honey pots.

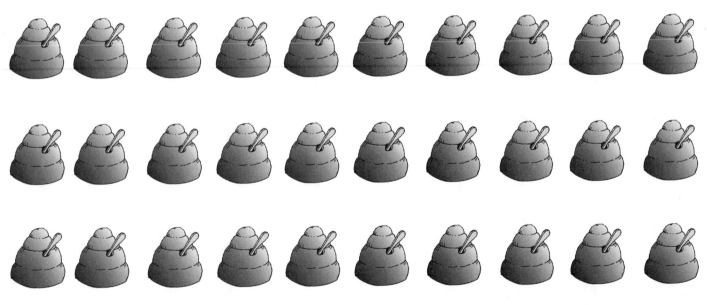

Count, read, and write whole numbers to 20

Number & Operations

One More, One Less, and In-between

Name _____

Trace the numbers.

1 2 3 4 5 6 7 8 9 10

11 12 13 14 15 16 17 18 19 20

Write the missing numbers.

in-between	one more	one less
8 __9__ 10	6 __7__	__2__ 3
3 ___ 5	11 ___	___ 9
12 ___ 14	9 ___	___ 11
6 ___ 8	15 ___	___ 20
10 ___ 12	7 ___	___ 13
18 ___ 20	4 ___	___ 7
15 ___ 17	19 ___	___ 17
12 ___ 14	14 ___	___ 12

Count, read, and write whole numbers to 20

8

EMC 3014 • Basic Math Skills, Grade 1 • ©2003 by Evan-Moor Corp.

Can You Help?

Someone bumped the calendar chart.
Some of the numbers fell on the floor.
Can you help put them back in order?

29 **4** **16**

February

Sunday	Monday	Tuesday	Wednesday	Thursday	Friday	Saturday
1		3	4		6	
	9		11			
15		17				21
22	23	24	25	26	27	28

8	20	2	13	16	7
5	12	18	10	19	14

Count, read, and write whole numbers to 20

Number & Operations

Name _____

Math Test

Fill in the circle next to the correct answer.

1. What number comes next?

9, 10, 11, 12, _____

Ⓐ 20
Ⓑ 15
Ⓒ 13
Ⓓ 8

2. What number is missing?

15, _____, 17, 18

Ⓐ 13
Ⓑ 16
Ⓒ 15
Ⓓ 20

3. Put these numbers in order.

19, 11, 20, 6, 15

Ⓐ 6, 15, 11, 19, 20
Ⓑ 6, 7, 8, 9, 10
Ⓒ 6, 11, 15, 19, 20
Ⓓ 6, 11, 19, 15, 20

4. Find the numbers that are NOT in order.

Ⓐ 12, 13, 14, 15, 16, 17
Ⓑ 9, 10, 12, 13, 14, 15
Ⓒ 6, 7, 8, 9, 10, 11
Ⓓ 15, 16, 17, 18, 19, 20

5. Which number is one more than 13?

Ⓐ 5
Ⓑ 14
Ⓒ 11
Ⓓ 8

6. Which number is one less than 13?

Ⓐ 14
Ⓑ 15
Ⓒ 12
Ⓓ 20

7. Which number is one less than 11?

Ⓐ 10
Ⓑ 12
Ⓒ 9
Ⓓ 1

8. Find the picture for 12.

Ⓐ

Ⓑ

Ⓒ

Ⓓ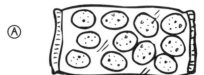

Count, read, and write whole numbers to 20

Guard on Duty

Name _____

Connect the dots from **1** to **50** to show what the soldier is guarding.

Count, read, and write whole numbers to 50

Number & Operations

Follow the Trail

Name _____

Write the missing numbers from **1** to **50** to help the donkey find his food.

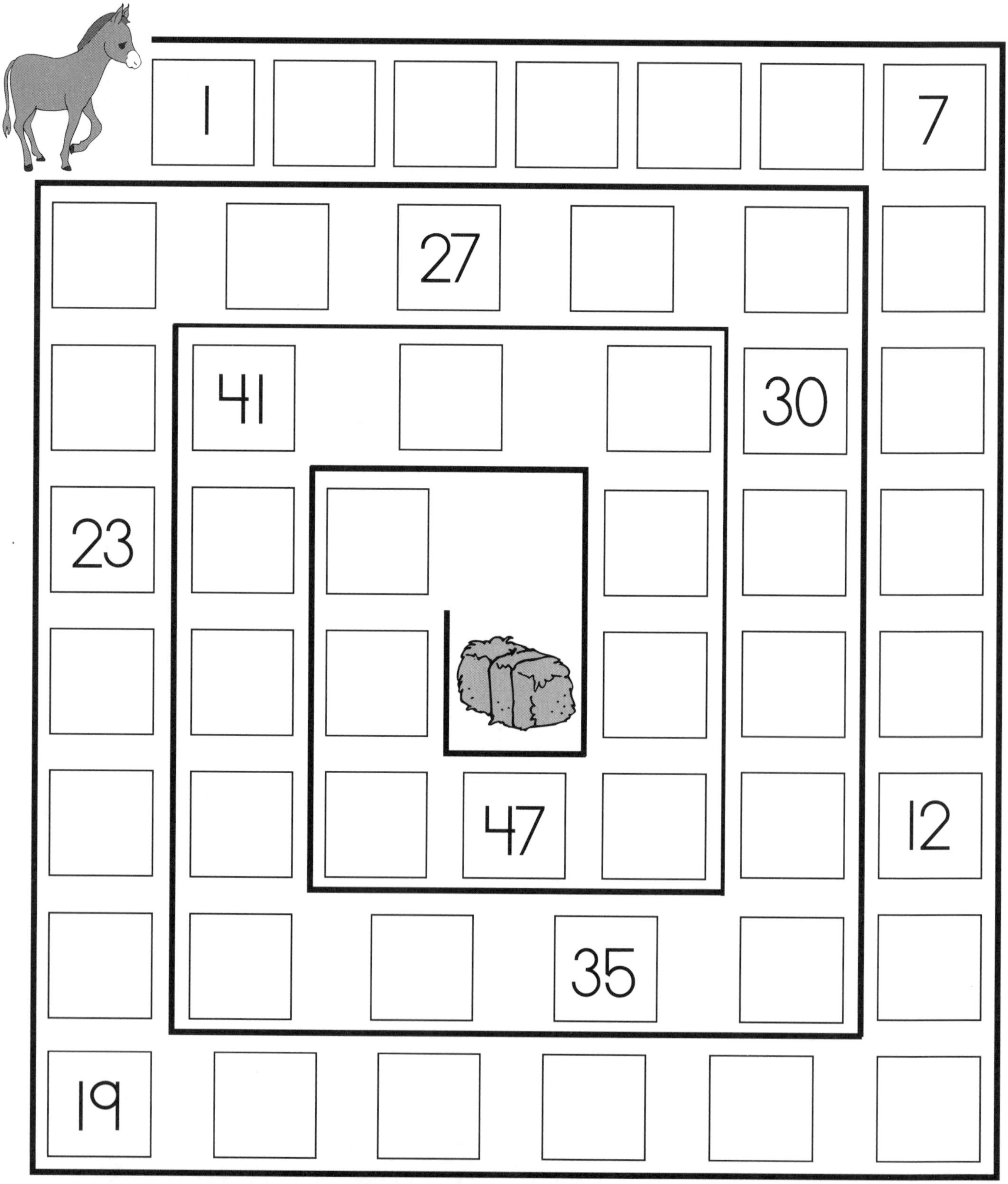

1						7

		27			
41				30	
23					
		47			12
			35		

19				

Count, read, and write whole numbers to 50

12

EMC 3014 • Basic Math Skills, Grade 1 • ©2003 by Evan-Moor Corp.

50 Puzzle Box

Name _____

Cut out the pieces.
Paste them in the box in order.

7 8 9 10

17 18 19 20

1 2 3 4 5 6

11 12 13 14 15 16

27 28

25 26

24

29 30

21 22 23

31 32 33

41 42 43

34 35 36 37

44 45 46 47

38 39 40

48 49 50

Count, read, and write whole numbers to 50

Number & Operations

One More, One Less, and In-between

Name _____

1	2	3	4	5	6	7	8	9	10
11	12	13	14	15	16	17	18	19	20
21	22	23	24	25	26	27	28	29	30
31	32	33	34	35	36	37	38	39	40
41	42	43	44	45	46	47	48	49	50

Write the missing numbers. Use the number chart.

in-between	one more	one less
1 2 3	9 10	9 10
11 ___ 13	19 ___	___ 30
37 ___ 39	29 ___	___ 50
19 ___ 21	39 ___	___ 27
48 ___ 50	49 ___	___ 43
25 ___ 27	16 ___	___ 9
44 ___ 46	27 ___	___ 46
32 ___ 34	31 ___	___ 32

Count, read, and write whole numbers to 50

Number & Operations — EMC 3014 • Basic Math Skills, Grade 1 • ©2003 by Evan-Moor Corp.

Class Count

Your job is to count things in your classroom.
Write the number by the picture.

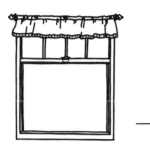 _____

 _____

 _____

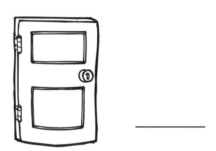 _____

 _____

 _____

 _____

 _____

Count, read, and write whole numbers to 50

Name _____

Fill in the circle next to the correct answer.

1. What number comes next?

36, 37, 38, 39, _____

Ⓐ 40
Ⓑ 30
Ⓒ 20
Ⓓ 50

2. What number is missing?

25, 26, _____, 28

Ⓐ 23
Ⓑ 26
Ⓒ 27
Ⓓ 29

3. What number is missing?

_____, 31, 32, 33

Ⓐ 35
Ⓑ 13
Ⓒ 40
Ⓓ 30

4. Find the numbers that are NOT in order.

Ⓐ 26, 27, 28, 29, 30
Ⓑ 45, 46, 47, 48, 49
Ⓒ 32, 31, 30, 33, 34
Ⓓ 36, 37, 38, 39, 40

5. Which number is one more than 30?

Ⓐ 25
Ⓑ 29
Ⓒ 19
Ⓓ 31

6. Which number is one less than 30?

Ⓐ 29
Ⓑ 45
Ⓒ 31
Ⓓ 37

7. Which number is one more than 11?

Ⓐ 20
Ⓑ 10
Ⓒ 13
Ⓓ 12

8. Which number is one less than 21?

Ⓐ 20
Ⓑ 22
Ⓒ 10
Ⓓ 2

Count, read, and write whole numbers to 50

EMC 3014 • Basic Math Skills, Grade 1 • ©2003 by Evan-Moor Corp.

A Strange Fish

Name _____

Start at **50**. Connect the dots in order.

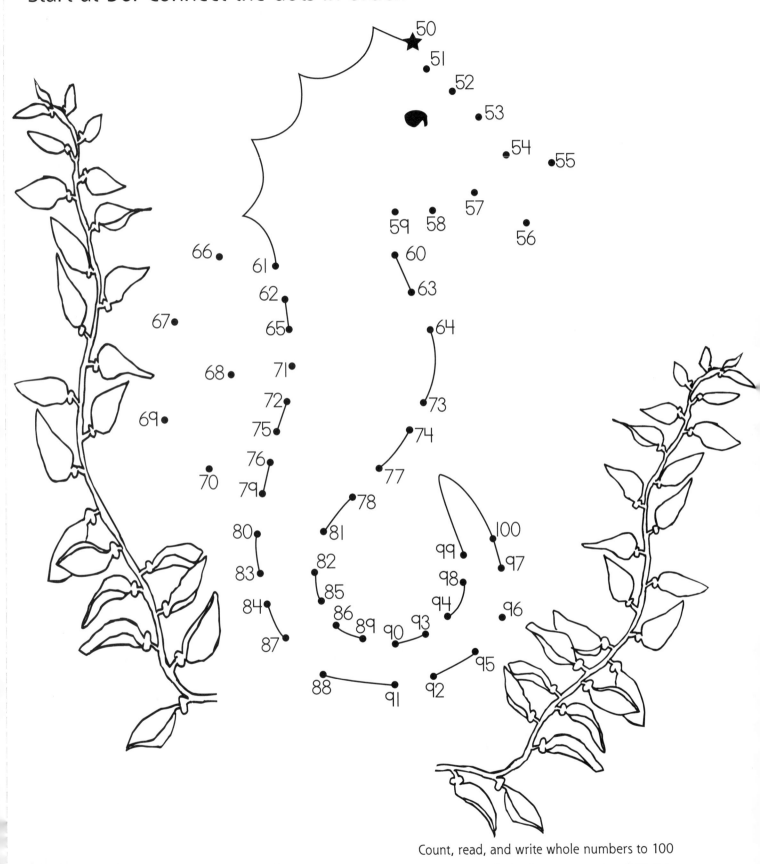

Number & Operations

I Want to Go Home!

Name _____

Help Baby Bear to his den.
Color the boxes green that count from **70** to **100**.

70	71	60	43	29	74	52	80
44	72	19	40	61	12	49	67
30	73	74	75	20	16	62	53
68	36	79	76	77	78	79	80
90	89	88	63	68	51	43	81
91	39	87	86	85	84	83	82
92	93	12	64	54	42	65	14
50	94	95	96	97	98	99	100

Count, read, and write whole numbers to 100

Number & Operations　　　　　　　　EMC 3014 • Basic Math Skills, Grade 1 • ©2003 by Evan-Moor Corp.

Count to 100

Name _____

Write numbers **1** to **100** in order.

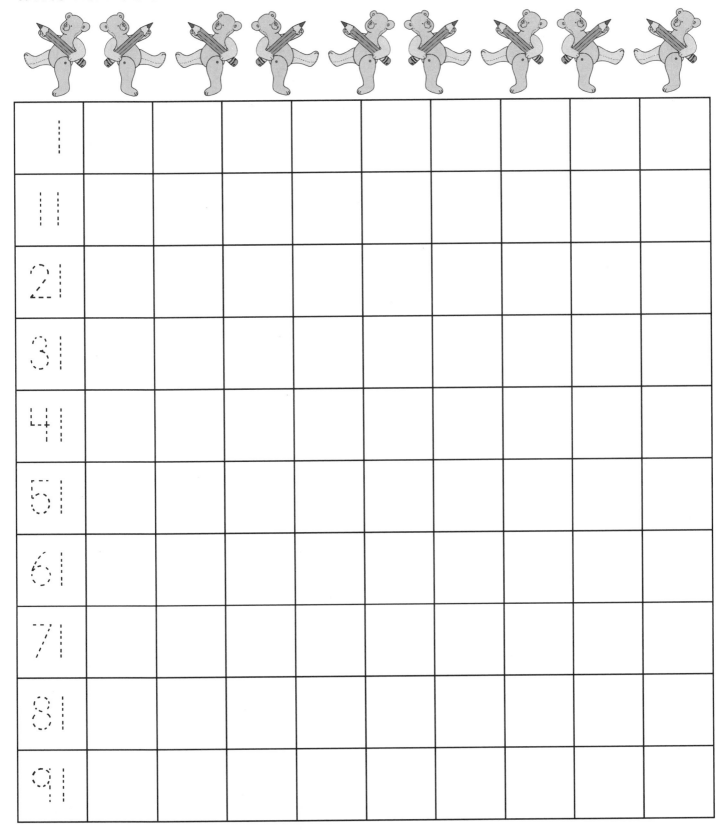

1									
11									
21									
31									
41									
51									
61									
71									
81									
91									

Count, read, and write whole numbers to 100

Number & Operations

More or Less?

1	2	3	4	5	6	7	8	9	10
11	12	13	14	15	16	17	18	19	20
21	22	23	24	25	26	27	28	29	30
31	32	33	34	35	36	37	38	39	40
41	42	43	44	45	46	47	48	49	50
51	52	53	54	55	56	57	58	59	60
61	62	63	64	65	66	67	68	69	70
71	72	73	74	75	76	77	78	79	80
81	82	83	84	85	86	87	88	89	90
91	92	93	94	95	96	97	98	99	100

Write the missing numbers. Use the number chart.

one more	one less	ten more	ten less
6 _7_	_2_ 3	6 _16_	_7_ 17
11 ___	___ 21	12 ___	___ 29
20 ___	___ 12	19 ___	___ 56
36 ___	___ 35	37 ___	___ 82
10 ___	___ 70	7 ___	___ 40
42 ___	___ 86	30 ___	___ 35
24 ___	___ 67	46 ___	___ 91
49 ___	___ 100	14 ___	___ 77

Count, read, and write whole numbers to 100

EMC 3014 • Basic Math Skills, Grade 1 • ©2003 by Evan-Moor Corp.

Who Has the Most Pennies?

Name _____

Maria, Kelly, and Tony save pennies.
Count on to see who has the most.

Maria has _____ pennies.

Kelly has _____ pennies.

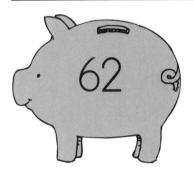

Tony has _____ pennies.

Who has the most pennies? _____

Count, read, and write whole numbers to 100

Math Test

Fill in the circle next to the correct answer.

1. What number comes next?

79, 80, 81, 82, _____

- Ⓐ 88
- Ⓑ 85
- Ⓒ 83
- Ⓓ 72

2. What number comes next?

96, 97, 98, 99, _____

- Ⓐ 95
- Ⓑ 90
- Ⓒ 10
- Ⓓ 100

3. What number is missing?

65, 66, 67, _____, 69, 70

- Ⓐ 62
- Ⓑ 66
- Ⓒ 57
- Ⓓ 68

4. Which number is one more than 95?

- Ⓐ 93
- Ⓑ 92
- Ⓒ 96
- Ⓓ 94

5. Which number is one less than 95?

- Ⓐ 94
- Ⓑ 95
- Ⓒ 97
- Ⓓ 99

6. Which number is ten more than 80?

- Ⓐ 70
- Ⓑ 80
- Ⓒ 90
- Ⓓ 60

7. Which number is ten less than 80?

- Ⓐ 70
- Ⓑ 80
- Ⓒ 90
- Ⓓ 60

8. Find the numbers that are NOT in order.

- Ⓐ 91, 92, 93, 94, 95
- Ⓑ 96, 97, 98, 99, 100
- Ⓒ 86, 87, 88, 90, 89
- Ⓓ 64, 65, 66, 67, 68

Count, read, and write whole numbers to 100

How Many Balls and Books?

Name _____

The children help Coach Brown put the balls away after recess.
Look at the ball each child is holding.
How many balls do you think will fill the box? Circle the number.

1.

basketball

2   12   50

2.

baseball

5   20   100

3.

beach ball

4   30   90

The children help their teacher put away books.

4. How many big books do you think
   will fill the shelf? _____

5. How many small books do you think
   will fill the shelf? _____

Make reasonable estimates when comparing larger or smaller numbers

Fill the Cup

Name _____

Circle the correct answer.

1. This is a jelly bean.

This is a cup.

About how many are in the cup?

    100   40   4

2. This is a marshmallow.

This is a cup.

About how many are in the cup?

    10   3   30

3. This is a crayon.

This is a cup.

About how many are in the cup?

    12   80   50

4. This is a peppermint candy.

This is a cup.

About how many are in the cup?

    4   24   100

Make reasonable estimates when comparing larger or smaller numbers

Number & Operations

EMC 3014 • Basic Math Skills, Grade 1 • ©2003 by Evan-Moor Corp.

Estimate How Many

Name _____

Circle the number that you think tells how many there are.

1. About how many strawberries?

2   15   100

2. About how many potatoes?

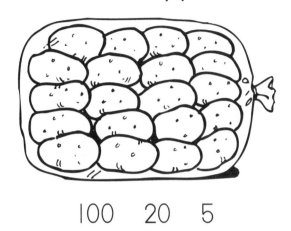

100   20   5

3. About how many paper clips?

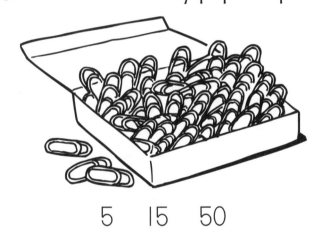

5   15   50

4. About how many balloons?

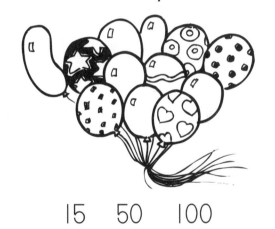

15   50   100

5. About how many peanuts?

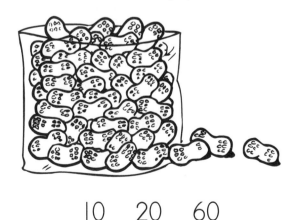

10   20   60

6. About how many apples?

30   60   6

Make reasonable estimates when comparing larger or smaller numbers

Number & Operations

More or Less?

Estimate how many. Circle the best answer.

1. About how many marshmallows are in the bag?

less than 30

more than 30

2. About how many cups of water will the jug hold?

less than 8

more than 8

3. About how many slices of bread are in the loaf?

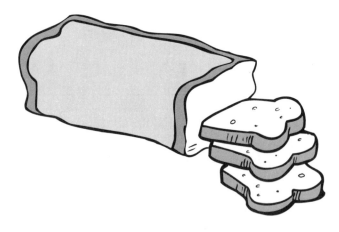

less than 9

more than 9

4. About how many blocks are in the box?

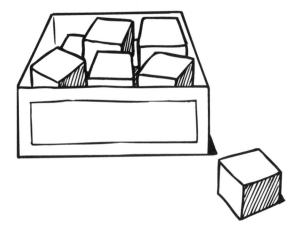

less than 20

more than 20

Make reasonable estimates when comparing larger or smaller numbers

Number & Operations   EMC 3014 • Basic Math Skills, Grade 1 • ©2003 by Evan-Moor Corp.

Plan a Party

Plan a party for all the first-graders in school.
Think about how much you need of each thing.
Write the numbers.

1.

_____ pizzas

2.

_____ jugs of juice

3.

_____ cartons of milk

4.

_____ bags of chips

5.

_____ apples

6.

_____ bags of cookies

Make reasonable estimates when comparing larger or smaller numbers

Name _____

Math Test

Fill in the circle next to the correct answer.

1. Which plate has about 12 cookies?

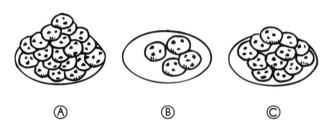

Ⓐ   Ⓑ   Ⓒ

2. Which bag has about 30 jelly beans?

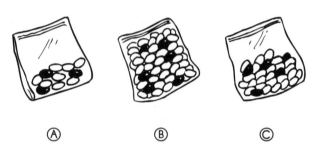

Ⓐ   Ⓑ   Ⓒ

3. Which cup has about 25 nuts?

Ⓐ   Ⓑ   Ⓒ

4. About how many toothpicks are in the box?

Ⓐ about 10
Ⓑ about 20
Ⓒ about 100

5. About how many eggs are in the nest?

Ⓐ less than 12
Ⓑ 12
Ⓒ more than 12

6. This cup has about _____ chips.

Ⓐ 10   Ⓑ 30   Ⓒ 100

7. About how much do I weigh?

Ⓐ   15 pounds
Ⓑ 100 pounds
Ⓒ   2 pounds

8. About how many pennies are in the jar?

Ⓐ   10 pennies
Ⓑ 100 pennies
Ⓒ   5 pennies

Make reasonable estimates when comparing larger or smaller numbers

Who Has More Cookies?

$$2 < 3$$
2 is **less than** 3

$$4 > 1$$
4 is **greater than** 1

Draw cookies to show how many. Then write **<** or **>** to compare the numbers.

1.
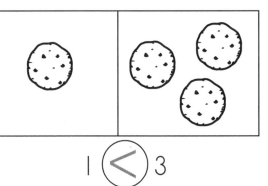

$$1 < 3$$

2.
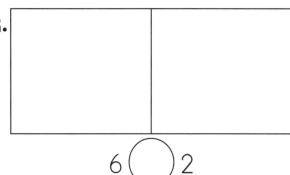

$$6 \bigcirc 2$$

3.
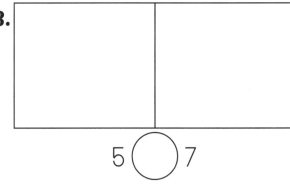

$$5 \bigcirc 7$$

4.
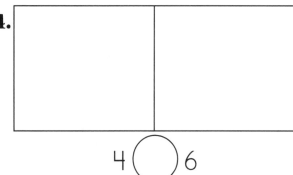

$$4 \bigcirc 6$$

5.
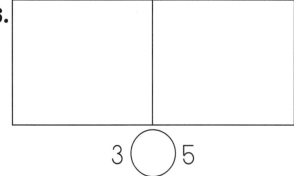

$$4 \bigcirc 2$$

6.

$$3 \bigcirc 5$$

Compare and order whole numbers to 100 using the symbols for less than, equal to, or greater than (<, =, >)

Balloons for Sale!

Name _____

13 is **less than** 50	80 is **greater than** 50
13 < 50	80 > 50

Color the balloons.

Use  for numbers **less than** 50.

Use other colors for numbers **greater than** 50.

Write < or >.

19 < 50   83 ◯ 50   51 ◯ 50   27 ◯ 50

64 ◯ 50   15 ◯ 50   49 ◯ 50   65 ◯ 50

Compare and order whole numbers to 100 using the symbols for less than, equal to, or greater than (<, =, >).

Greater, Less, or Equal?

25 (>) 10	39 (<) 50	15 (=) 15

Use **>**, **<**, or **=**.

1. 8 (>) 6   14 ( ) 19   26 ( ) 26

2. 43 ( ) 40   15 ( ) 51   90 ( ) 89

3. 37 ( ) 73   21 ( ) 12   48 ( ) 44

4. 100 ( ) 99   71 ( ) 74   77 ( ) 77

5. Write a number that is greater than 25.   _____

6. Write a number that is less than 52.   _____

7. Write a number that is equal to 99.

Compare and order whole numbers to 100 using the symbols for less than, equal to, or greater than (<, =, >)

Number & Operations

Greater Than or Less Than?

Name _____

Write a number to make the statement true.
Use different numbers each time.

greater than

1. __7__ > 6

2. _____ > 21

3. _____ > 40

4. _____ > 67

5. _____ > 83

6. _____ > 99

less than

7. __5__ < 6

8. _____ < 21

9. _____ < 40

10. _____ < 67

11. _____ < 83

12. _____ < 99

Circle the answer.

1. 1, 7, 3, 12, 9, 4
   All these numbers are _____ 15.   < = >

2. 17, 20, 18, 51, 26
   All these numbers are _____ 15.   < = >

3. 90, 70, 100, 80
   All these numbers are _____ 50.   < = >

4. 10, 30, 20, 40
   All these numbers are _____ 50.   < = >

Compare and order whole numbers to 100 using the symbols for less than, equal to, or greater than (<, =, >).

EMC 3014 • Basic Math Skills, Grade 1 • ©2003 by Evan-Moor Corp.

The Winner!

Name _____

1. Ali and Bo played a game of cards. Ali made 18 points. Bo made 16 points. Who won the game?

_____ won

18 points ◯ 16 points

2. Anita and Jamal played a game of marbles. Anita got 15 marbles. Jamal got 27 marbles. Who won the game?

_____ won

15 marbles ◯ 27 marbles

3. Raul and Tom were in a fishing contest. Raul caught 8 fish. Tom caught 11 fish. Who won the contest?

_____ won

8 fish ◯ 11 fish

4. Meg and Mia were in a contest. The person who sold the most cookies won a prize. Meg sold 53 boxes of cookies. Mia sold 35 boxes of cookies. Who won the prize?

_____ won

53 boxes ◯ 35 boxes

5. Write a word problem about this picture. Write the answer.

Scoreboard	
Tigers	Bears
21	18

_____

_____

_____

____ ◯ ____   _____ won

Compare and order whole numbers to 100 using the symbols for less than, equal to, or greater than (<, =, >)

Number & Operations

Math Test

Fill in the circle next to the correct answer.

1. Which number is more than 75?

Ⓐ 72

Ⓑ 55

Ⓒ 70

Ⓓ 80

2. Which number is more than 50?

Ⓐ 30

Ⓑ 29

Ⓒ 51

Ⓓ 48

3. Which symbol is missing?

16 ◯ 25

Ⓐ <

Ⓑ >

Ⓒ =

4. Which symbol is missing?

69 ◯ 31

Ⓐ <

Ⓑ >

Ⓒ =

5. Which number is missing?

20 < _____

Ⓐ 15   Ⓑ 11   Ⓒ 27   Ⓓ 12

6. Which number is missing?

15 = _____

Ⓐ 18   Ⓑ 51   Ⓒ 5   Ⓓ 15

7. Tammy has 5 goldfish. She has 3 cats. Which of these tells about her pets?

Ⓐ 5 goldfish > 3 cats

Ⓑ 5 goldfish < 3 cats

Ⓒ 5 goldfish = 3 cats

Ⓓ 3 cats > 5 goldfish

8. Mark has 52 pennies. Jacob has 59 pennies. Which of these tells about the pennies?

Ⓐ 52 pennies > 59 pennies

Ⓑ 52 pennies = 59 pennies

Ⓒ 52 pennies < 59 pennies

Ⓓ 59 pennies < 52 pennies

Compare and order whole numbers to 100 using the symbols for less than, equal to, or greater than (<, =, >).

Catch the Rabbits

Name _____

A cage holds 10 rabbits.
Circle groups of **10** rabbits for each cage.
Count how many rabbits are left.

1. How many full cages are there? _____

   How many rabbits are left? _____

2. How many full cages are there? _____

   How many rabbits are left? _____

3. How many full cages are there? _____

   How many rabbits are left? _____

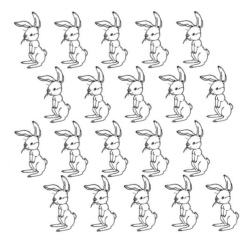

Count and group objects in tens and ones

Number & Operations

Count the Kittens

Name _____

Count the kittens to find the answer.

1 **ten** =    1 **one** = 🐱

1.

___1___ ten ___4___ ones

How many kittens in all? _____

2.

_____ tens _____ ones

How many kittens in all? _____

3.

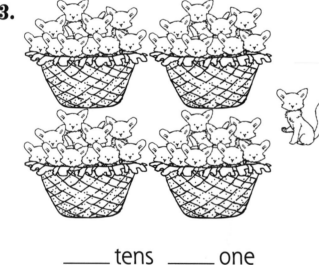

_____ tens _____ one

How many kittens in all? _____

4.

_____ ten _____ ones

How many kittens in all? _____

Count and group objects in tens and ones

Number & Operations

EMC 3014 • Basic Math Skills, Grade 1 • ©2003 by Evan-Moor Corp.

Tens and Ones ✓

Name _Annee Bess_

Each block is one.
Here are 3 **ones**.

Each stack has 10 blocks.
This is 1 **ten**.

Count the **tens** and **ones**.
Write how many blocks in all.

1.

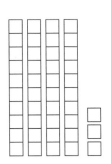

_4_ _3_ = _____
tens ones   in all

2.

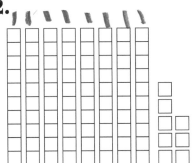

_8_ _8_ = _88_
tens ones   in all

3.

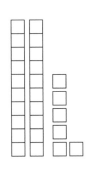

_2_ _____ = _____
tens ones   in all

4.

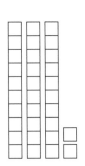

_____ _____ = _____
tens ones   in all

5.

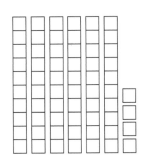

_____ _____ = _____
tens ones   in all

6.

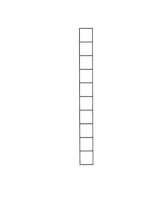

_____ _____ = _____
ten ones   in all

Count and group objects in tens and ones

Bowls of Cherries

Name _____

 = 1 one	 = 1 ten

<u>2</u>   <u>3</u>   <u>23</u>
tens ones in all

_____ _____ _____
tens ones in all

_____ _____ _____
tens ones in all

_____ _____ _____
tens ones in all

_____ _____ _____
tens ones in all

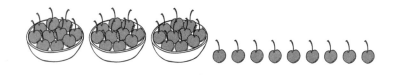

_____ _____ _____
tens ones in all

Finish the table.

Tens	Ones	In All
5	5	_____
9	7	_____
6	3	_____

Count and group objects in tens and ones

EMC 3014 • Basic Math Skills, Grade 1 • ©2003 by Evan-Moor Corp.

Dimes and Pennies

Count the tens and ones.
Write how many cents in all.

ten	one
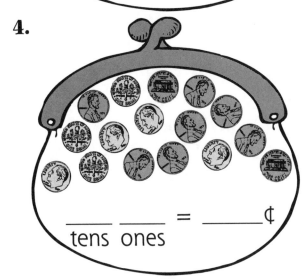	

1.

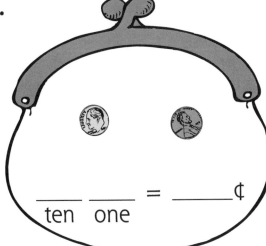

____ ____ = _____¢
ten one

2.

____ ____ = _____¢
tens ones

3.

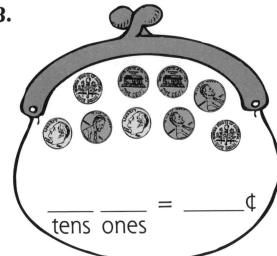

____ ____ = _____¢
tens ones

4.

____ ____ = _____¢
tens ones

5.

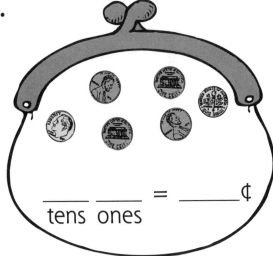

____ ____ = _____¢
tens ones

6.

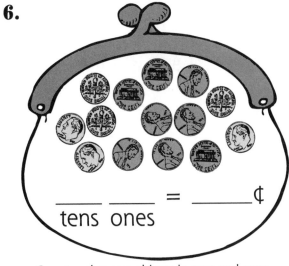

____ ____ = _____¢
tens ones

Count and group objects in tens and ones

Number & Operations

Math Test

Fill in the circle next to the correct answer.

1. How many ones?

Ⓐ 2
Ⓑ 3
Ⓒ 7
Ⓓ 5

2. How many tens?

Ⓐ 33
Ⓑ 4
Ⓒ 3
Ⓓ 20

3. How many tens?

Ⓐ 8
Ⓑ 5
Ⓒ 6
Ⓓ 7

4. Which number has 4 tens and 8 ones?

Ⓐ 18
Ⓑ 84
Ⓒ 48
Ⓓ 12

5. Which number has 6 tens and 0 ones?

Ⓐ 610
Ⓑ 63
Ⓒ 6
Ⓓ 60

6. How many tens and ones are in 57?

Ⓐ 5 ones and 7 tens
Ⓑ 5 tens and 7 ones
Ⓒ 5 tens and 7 tens
Ⓓ 7 ones and 5 ones

7. What is the number for this picture?

Ⓐ 15
Ⓑ 52
Ⓒ 30
Ⓓ 25

8. What is the number for this picture?

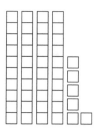

Ⓐ 46
Ⓑ 64
Ⓒ 36
Ⓓ 100

Count and group objects in tens and ones

EMC 3014 • Basic Math Skills, Grade 1 • ©2003 by Evan-Moor Corp.

What Is It?

Count by **tens** to **100**.

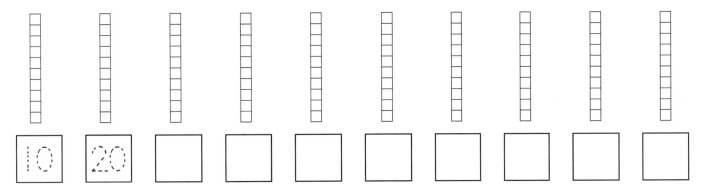

Count by **tens**. Connect the dots from **10** to **100** in order.

30

20

70
100

80

40

90

50

60

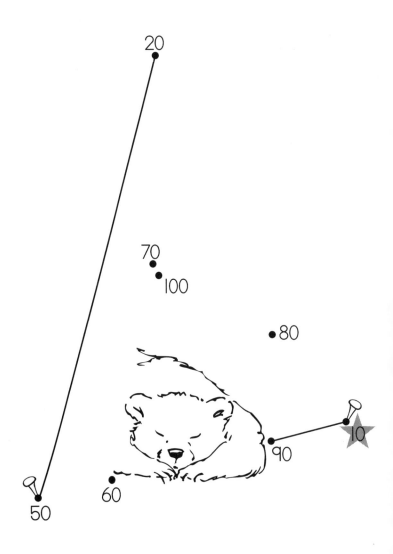

10

Count by 10s to 100

Number & Operations

Find the Tens

Count by **tens** to **100**.

10	20								

Use  gray or brown to color the shapes that have the numbers you wrote.

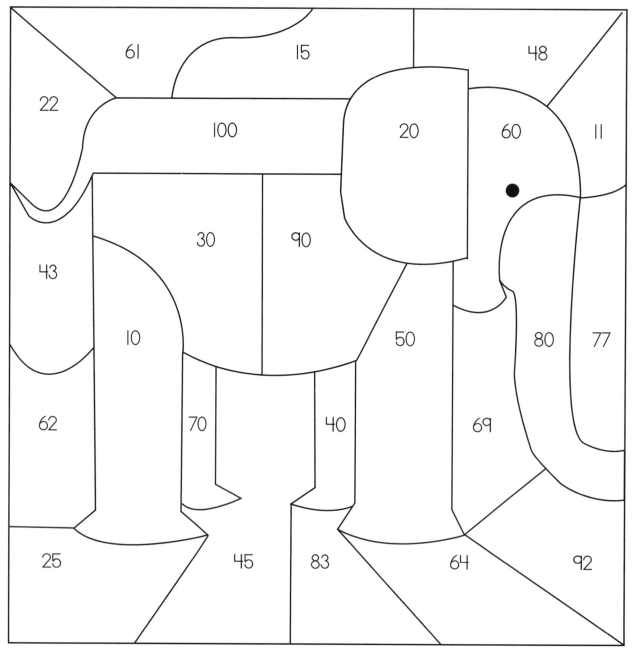

Count by 10s to 100

How Many Tens in 100?

Name _____

Count by **tens** and color those boxes.
Count the boxes you colored.

1	2	3	4	5	6	7	8	9	10
11	12	13	14	15	16	17	18	19	20
21	22	23	24	25	26	27	28	29	30
31	32	33	34	35	36	37	38	39	40
41	42	43	44	45	46	47	48	49	50
51	52	53	54	55	56	57	58	59	60
61	62	63	64	65	66	67	68	69	70
71	72	73	74	75	76	77	78	79	80
81	82	83	84	85	86	87	88	89	90
91	92	93	94	95	96	97	98	99	100

How many **tens** are in **100**? _____ tens

Count by 10s to 100

Bananas for Monkeys

Name _____

Help the monkeys get to the bananas.
Count by **10s** to fill in the missing numbers.

Count by 10s to 100

EMC 3014 • Basic Math Skills, Grade 1 • ©2003 by Evan-Moor Corp.

What Is the Number?

10 20 30 40 50 60 70 80 90 100

1. Count by tens. Go past 30 but not past 50. What is the number? _____	**2.** Count by tens. I am between 80 and 100. What is the number? _____
3. Count by tens. I am ten more than 70. What is the number? _____	**4.** Count by tens. I am after 20 but before 40. What is the number? _____
5. Count by tens. I am the next ten after 50. What is the number? _____	**6.** Count by tens. I am the number of cents equal to 7 dimes. What is the number? _____

Count by 10s to 100

Number & Operations

Name _____

Fill in the circle next to the correct answer.

1. What number comes next in this pattern?

   70, 80, 90, ____

   Ⓐ 60
   Ⓑ 40
   Ⓒ 100
   Ⓓ 95

2. What is the missing number in this pattern?

   20, 30, ____, 50

   Ⓐ 40
   Ⓑ 20
   Ⓒ 30
   Ⓓ 10

3. What is the missing number in this pattern?

   50, ____, 70, 80

   Ⓐ 90   Ⓑ 100   Ⓒ 40   Ⓓ 60

4. Put these numbers in order.

   50, 70, 90, 60, 80

   Ⓐ 50, 55, 60, 65, 70
   Ⓑ 70, 80, 90, 50, 60
   Ⓒ 50, 60, 70, 80, 90
   Ⓓ 50, 60, 90, 70, 80

5. Which number does NOT belong?

   10, 20, 25, 30

   Ⓐ 25
   Ⓑ 30
   Ⓒ 20
   Ⓓ 10

6. Which number is in the wrong place?

   50, 60, 30, 70

   Ⓐ 50
   Ⓑ 60
   Ⓒ 70
   Ⓓ 30

7. One dime is 10¢. How much is 3 dimes?

   Ⓐ 10¢
   Ⓑ 20¢
   Ⓒ 30¢
   Ⓓ 40¢

8. There are 10 peanuts in each bag. How many peanuts are there in all?

   Ⓐ 40   Ⓑ 80   Ⓒ 50   Ⓓ 70

Who Is It?

Name _____

Count by **5s**.

𝍸	𝍸	𝍸	𝍸	𝍸	𝍸	𝍸	𝍸	𝍸	𝍸

5 ___ ___ ___ ___ ___ ___ ___ ___ ___

𝍸	𝍸	𝍸	𝍸	𝍸	𝍸	𝍸	𝍸	𝍸	𝍸

___ ___ ___ ___ ___ ___ ___ ___ ___ ___

Count by **5s** to connect the dots.

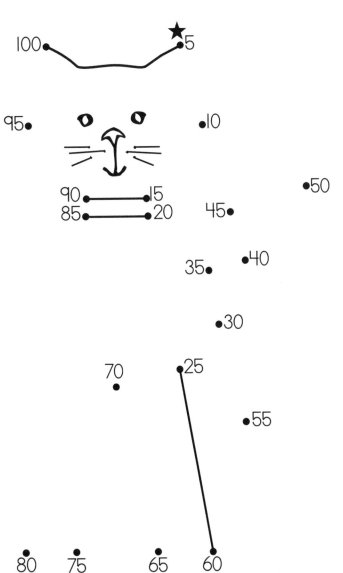

Count by 5s to 100

Number & Operations

Through the Woods

Count by **5s** to get to the lake.
Fill in the missing numbers.

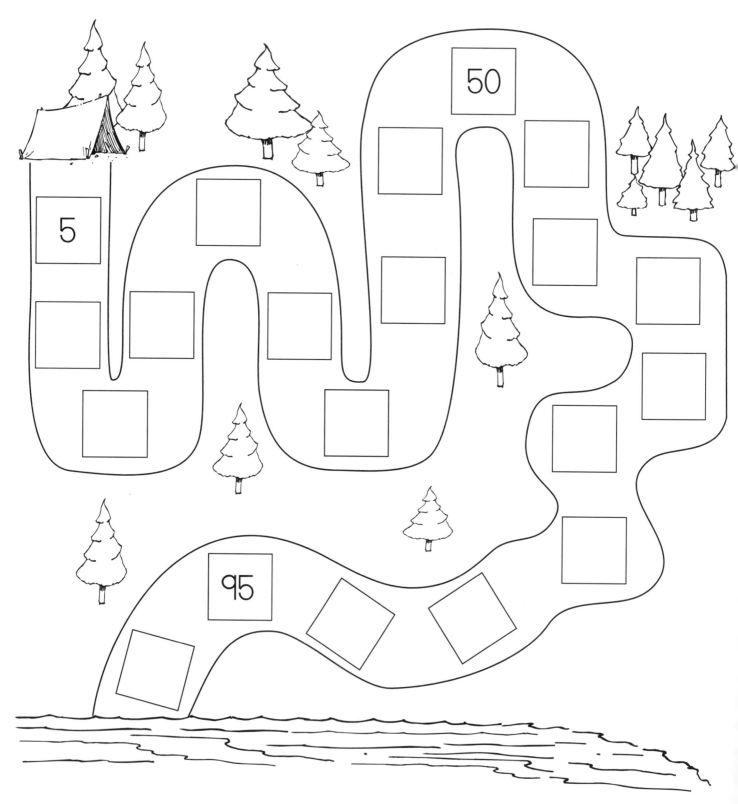

Count by 5s to 100

Number & Operations

EMC 3014 • Basic Math Skills, Grade 1 • ©2003 by Evan-Moor Corp.

Count by Fives

Circle the boxes you need to count by **fives** to **100**.

Use 🖍 red 🖍 to color the boxes you circled.

Use 🖍 yellow 🖍 to color the rest of the boxes.

1	2	3	4	(5)	6	7	8	9	(10)
11	12	13	14	15	16	17	18	19	20
21	22	23	24	25	26	27	28	29	30
31	32	33	34	35	36	37	38	39	40
41	42	43	44	45	46	47	48	49	50
51	52	53	54	55	56	57	58	59	60
61	62	63	64	65	66	67	68	69	70
71	72	73	74	75	76	77	78	79	80
81	82	83	84	85	86	87	88	89	90
91	92	93	94	95	96	97	98	99	100

Count by **fives** to **100**. Write the numbers in order.

5   10   ___   ___   ___   ___   ___   ___   ___

___   ___   ___   ___   ___   ___   ___   ___

Count by 5s to 100

Five Cents

A nickel is five cents. Count these nickels by **fives** to see how much money is in the box.

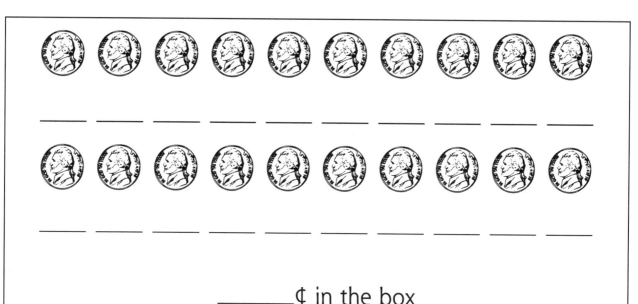

_____ _____ _____ _____ _____ _____ _____ _____ _____ _____

_____ _____ _____ _____ _____ _____ _____ _____ _____ _____

_____¢ in the box

Write the numbers in order.

10   5   20   15   ____ ____ ____ ____

55   45   40. 50   ____ ____ ____ ____

95   85   100   90   ____ ____ ____ ____

Count by 5s to 100

Count by Fives

Name _____

Draw pictures to help you answer the questions. Then count by **fives**.

1. Raul has 5 boxes. He puts 5 nuts in each box. How many nuts does he have in all?

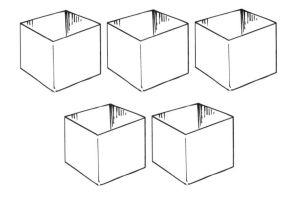

_____ nuts

2. Kelly has 3 vases. She puts 5 flowers in each vase. How many flowers does she have in all?

_____ flowers

3. Angelo has 12 nickels in his bank. He takes out 5 nickels. How much money is left in his bank?

_____ ¢

4. Mr. Williams sells pet fish. He has 8 bowls. He puts 5 fish in each bowl. How many fish does Mr. Williams have to sell?

_____ fish

Count by 5s to 100

Number & Operations

Math Test

Fill in the circle next to the correct answer.

1. Put these numbers in order.
   15, 10, 5, 20, 25

   Ⓐ 10, 20, 25, 15, 5
   Ⓑ 10, 15, 20, 25, 5
   Ⓒ 5, 10, 15, 20, 25
   Ⓓ 5, 10, 20, 15, 25

2. What number comes next in this pattern?
   50, 55, 60, 65, _____

   Ⓐ 66
   Ⓑ 75
   Ⓒ 80
   Ⓓ 70

3. What number is missing in this pattern?
   50, 55, _____, 65, 70

   Ⓐ 45
   Ⓑ 60
   Ⓒ 50
   Ⓓ 75

4. What number is missing in this pattern?
   15, 20, 25, _____, 35

   Ⓐ 25   Ⓑ 45   Ⓒ 26   Ⓓ 30

5. Which number does NOT belong?
   15, 20, 25, 33, 35

   Ⓐ 15
   Ⓑ 33
   Ⓒ 35
   Ⓓ 25

6. Which number does NOT belong?
   65, 70, 75, 80, 25, 85

   Ⓐ 65
   Ⓑ 80
   Ⓒ 85
   Ⓓ 25

7. One nickel is 5¢. How much is 3 nickels?
   Ⓐ 10¢
   Ⓑ 15¢
   Ⓒ 25¢
   Ⓓ 20¢

8. Each bucket holds 5 cups of sand. How many cups of sand are in 8 buckets?

   Ⓐ 35   Ⓑ 60   Ⓒ 40   Ⓓ 20

Count by 5s to 100

Shoe Sale

Name _____

How many shoes are there in the sale?
Count by **twos**. Write the numbers on the lines.
Color the pair of shoes you would buy at the shoe sale.

2   4   ___   ___   ___

Count by 2s to 100

A Thirsty Zebra

Name _____

The zebra wants a drink of water.
Show the path to the water.
Count by **twos**. Color those boxes.

2	4	6	3	9	11	0
13	17	8	15	11	19	5
14	12	10	21	38	40	42
16	13	23	34	36	24	44
18	20	31	32	35	25	46
19	22	27	30	39	27	48
21	24	26	28	37	16	50

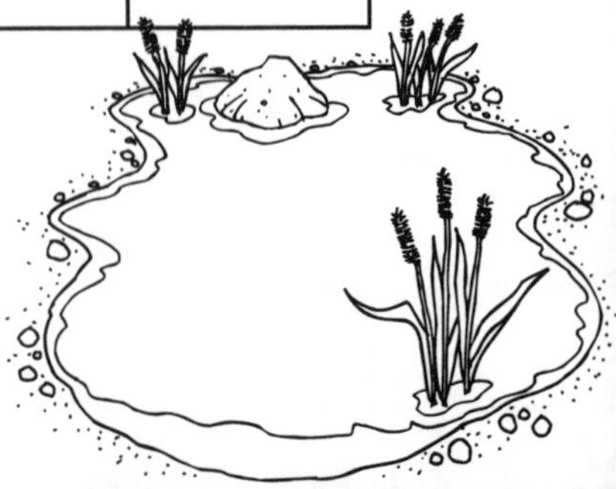

Count by 2s to 100

EMC 3014 • Basic Math Skills, Grade 1 • ©2003 by Evan-Moor Corp.

Count by Twos

Name _____

Count by **twos**. Color those numbers **blue**.

1	2	3	4	5	6	7	8	9	10
11	12	13	14	15	16	17	18	19	20
21	22	23	24	25	26	27	28	29	30
31	32	33	34	35	36	37	38	39	40
41	42	43	44	45	46	47	48	49	50
51	52	53	54	55	56	57	58	59	60
61	62	63	64	65	66	67	68	69	70
71	72	73	74	75	76	77	78	79	80
81	82	83	84	85	86	87	88	89	90
91	92	93	94	95	96	97	98	99	100

Count by 2s to 100

Number & Operations

Count by Twos

Count by **twos**. Write the missing numbers.

2 ____ ____ ____ ____ 10

12 ____ ____ ____ ____ 20

22 ____ ____ ____ 28 ____

32 ____ 36 ____ ____

42 ____ ____ ____ 50

52 ____ 56 ____ ____

62 ____ ____ 68 ____

72 ____ ____ ____ 80

82 ____ ____ 88 ____

92 ____ ____ ____ ____

Count by 2s to 100

Number & Operations

Helping Father

Name _____

Help Father get ready for a sale at his store.
Circle groups of two things. Then count by **twos**.

1. Circle groups of two mittens.

   How many mittens in all? _____

_____

2. Circle groups of two socks.

   How many socks in all? _____

_____

3. Circle groups of two shoes.

   How many shoes in all? _____

_____

Now try this.
Count by **twos** to see how many socks and shoes
in your classroom.

_____ shoes   _____ socks

Count by 2s to 100

Number & Operations

Name _____

Fill in the circle next to the correct answer.

1. How many mittens?

- Ⓐ 4
- Ⓑ 6
- Ⓒ 8
- Ⓓ 10

2. How many boots?

- Ⓐ 6
- Ⓑ 16
- Ⓒ 14
- Ⓓ 12

3. How many socks?

- Ⓐ 24
- Ⓑ 18
- Ⓒ 10
- Ⓓ 20

4. What number comes next in this pattern?

16, 18, _____

- Ⓐ 10
- Ⓑ 20
- Ⓒ 30
- Ⓓ 40

Count by 2s to 100

5. What number comes next in this pattern?

26, 28, 30, _____

- Ⓐ 49
- Ⓑ 38
- Ⓒ 30
- Ⓓ 32

6. Put these numbers in order.

16, 20, 18, 22

- Ⓐ 16, 22, 18, 20
- Ⓑ 20, 22, 16, 18
- Ⓒ 20, 16, 18, 22
- Ⓓ 16, 18, 20, 22

7. Put these numbers in order.

88, 90, 86, 92

- Ⓐ 86, 88, 92, 90
- Ⓑ 90, 92, 88, 86
- Ⓒ 86, 88, 90, 92
- Ⓓ 88, 86, 90, 92

8. Which number does NOT belong?

26, 28, 30, 31, 32

- Ⓐ 31
- Ⓑ 32
- Ⓒ 30
- Ⓓ 28

EMC 3014 • Basic Math Skills, Grade 1 • ©2003 by Evan-Moor Corp.

In My Piggy Bank

Name _____

Color the pennies brown. Draw an **X** on the nickels.
Circle the dimes.

Count the coins. Count by **ones**, **fives**, or **tens**. Then write how much money you have.

_____ pennies = _____¢

_____ nickels = _____¢

_____ dimes = _____¢

Identify and know the value of coins (penny, nickel, dime) and show different combinations of coins that equal the same value

Find the Surprise

Count the money. Color shapes with **1¢** red.
Color shapes with **5¢** yellow. Color shapes with **10¢** blue.

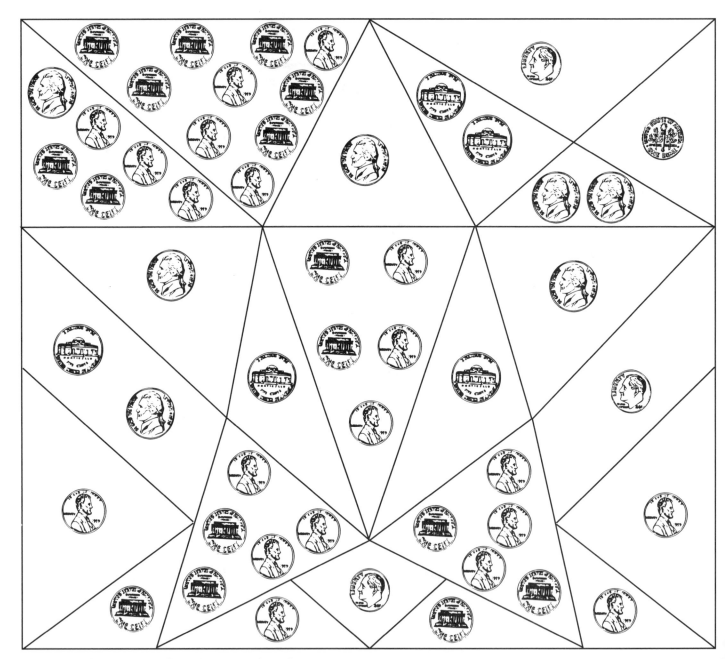

What did you find? Circle the answer.

Identify and know the value of coins (penny, nickel, dime) and show different combinations of coins that equal the same value

How Much Money?

Name _____

Count on. Write the amount.

10 11 12 13 13¢

1.  _____ ¢

10 11

2.  _____ ¢

3.  _____ ¢

4. _____ ¢

5. _____ ¢

6.  _____ ¢

7.  _____ ¢

8.  _____ ¢

Identify and know the value of coins (penny, nickel, dime) and show different combinations of coins that equal the same value

Number & Operations

The Same Amount

Name _____

Show each amount of money two ways.
Cut out the coins. Paste them in the boxes.

10¢		
35¢		
40¢		

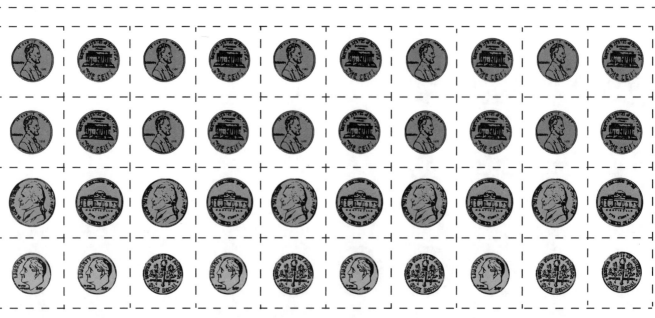

Identify and know the value of coins (penny, nickel, dime) and show different combinations of coins that equal the same value

Number & Operations   EMC 3014 • Basic Math Skills, Grade 1 • ©2003 by Evan-Moor Corp.

Ice-Cream Treats

10¢   15¢   20¢

Circle what you need. Then write the amounts.

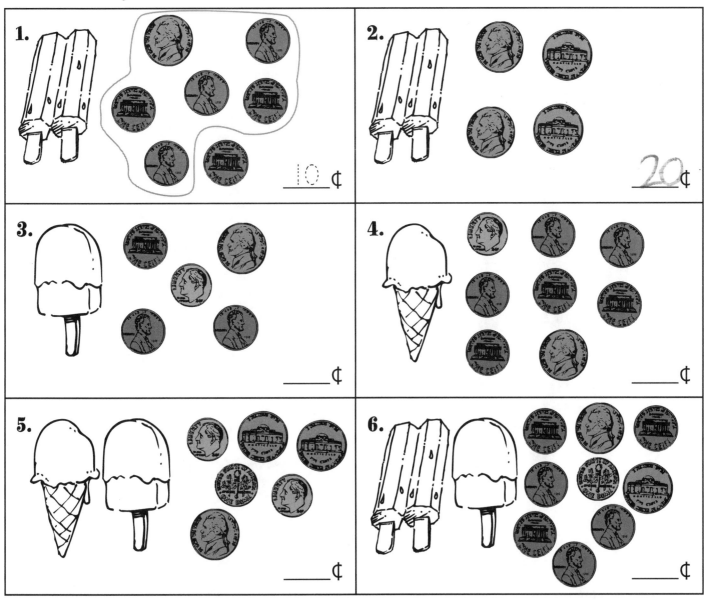

1. _10_ ¢

2. _20_ ¢

3. _____ ¢

4. _____ ¢

5. _____ ¢

6. _____ ¢

Identify and know the value of coins (penny, nickel, dime) and show different combinations of coins that equal the same value

Math Test

Fill in the circle next to the correct answer.

1. What is the name of this coin?

Ⓐ dime

Ⓑ dollar

Ⓒ nickel

Ⓓ penny

2. What is the name of this coin?

Ⓐ penny

Ⓑ nickel

Ⓒ dime

Ⓓ dollar

3. What is the name of this coin?

Ⓐ nickel

Ⓑ dollar

Ⓒ dime

Ⓓ penny

4. Which coin is worth 5¢?

Ⓐ   Ⓑ   Ⓒ   Ⓓ

5. Which coin is worth 10¢?

Ⓐ   Ⓑ   Ⓒ   Ⓓ

6. How much money is this?

Ⓐ 5¢   Ⓑ 10¢   Ⓒ 15¢   Ⓓ 20¢

7. Which shows the same amount?

Ⓐ   Ⓑ   Ⓒ   Ⓓ

8. Which coins show the money needed to buy this toy?

Ⓐ

Ⓑ

Ⓒ

Ⓓ

Identify and know the value of coins (penny, nickel, dime) and show different combinations of coins that equal the same value

Tic-Tac-Toe

Play Tic-Tac-Toe. Draw **X** or **O**.

X—25¢   **O**—40¢

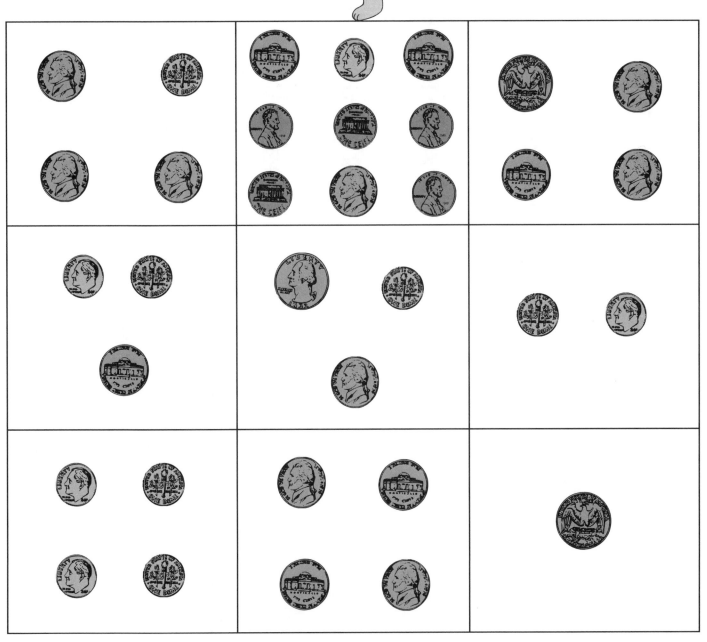

Who won?   **X** or **O**

Identify and know the value of coins (penny, nickel, dime, quarter) and show different combinations of coins that equal the same value

Color the Rug

Name _____

25¢ blue   18¢ green   30¢ red

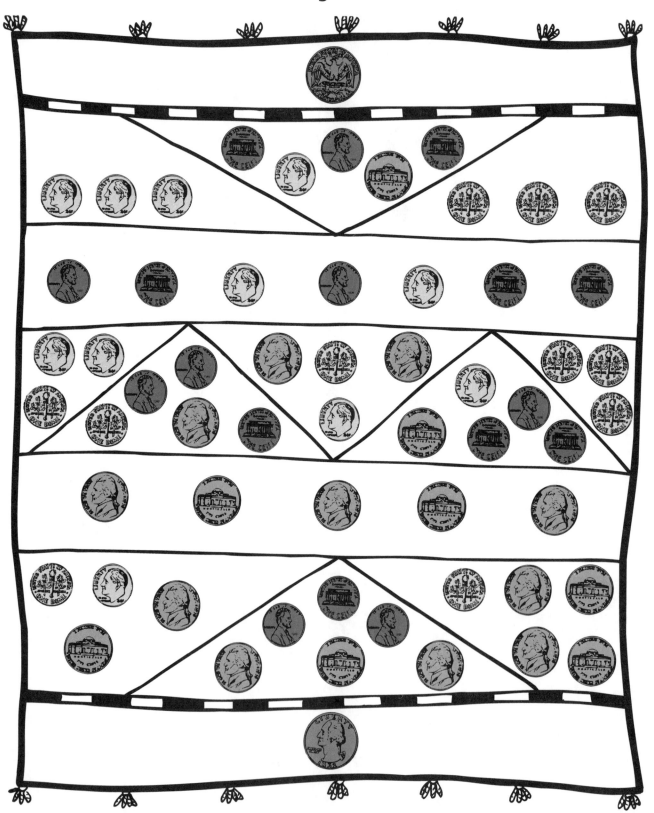

Identify and know the value of coins (penny, nickel, dime, quarter) and show different combinations of coins that equal the same value

EMC 3014 • Basic Math Skills, Grade 1 • ©2003 by Evan-Moor Corp.

How Much Is It?

Match coins and amounts.

28¢

12¢

25¢

26¢

19¢

50¢

34¢

40¢

Draw an **X** on the most money.

Identify and know the value of coins (penny, nickel, dime, quarter) and show different combinations of coins that equal the same value

Toys for Sale

Can you buy the toy? Write how much money you have.
Then circle **yes** or **no**.

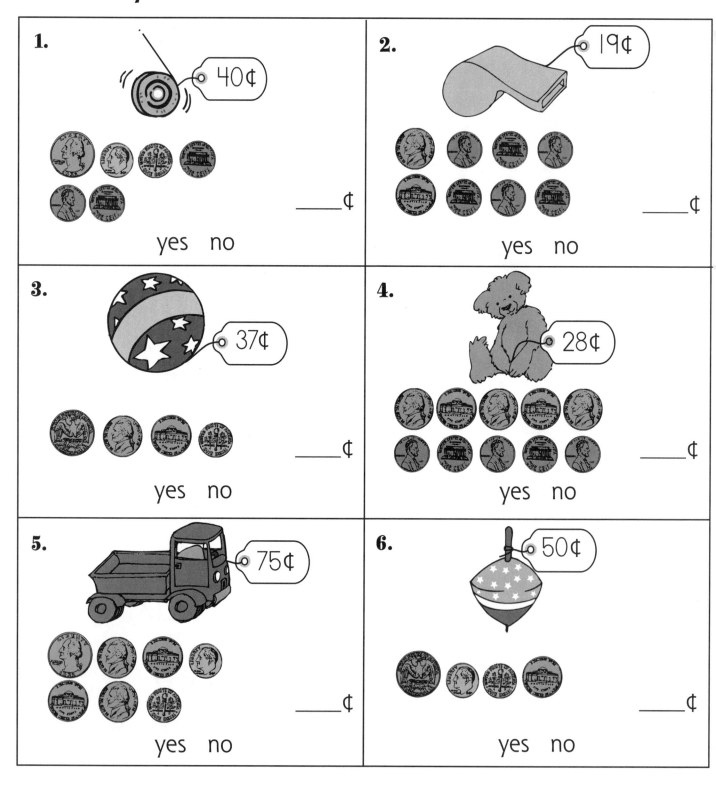

1.

40¢

_____ ¢

yes   no

2.

19¢

_____ ¢

yes   no

3.

37¢

_____ ¢

yes   no

4.

28¢

_____ ¢

yes   no

5.

75¢

_____ ¢

yes   no

6.

50¢

_____ ¢

yes   no

Identify and know the value of coins (penny, nickel, dime, quarter) and show different combinations of coins that equal the same value

EMC 3014 • Basic Math Skills, Grade 1 • ©2003 by Evan-Moor Corp.

Nuts for Sale!

Name _____

Peanut 5¢   Acorn 10¢   Walnut 15¢

How much do these nuts cost?

1. _____ ¢

2. _____ ¢

3. _____ ¢

4.  _____ ¢

5.  _____ ¢

6. Draw the nuts you would buy if you had a quarter.

Identify and know the value of coins (penny, nickel, dime, quarter) and show different combinations of coins that equal the same value

Name _____

Fill in the circle next to the correct answer.

1. What is the name of this coin?
    Ⓐ nickel
    Ⓑ quarter
    Ⓒ dime
    Ⓓ penny

2. How do you count nickels?
    Ⓐ Count by tens.
    Ⓑ Count by ones.
    Ⓒ Count by twos.
    Ⓓ Count by fives.

3. How do you count dimes?
    Ⓐ Count by ones.
    Ⓑ Count by twos.
    Ⓒ Count by fives.
    Ⓓ Count by tens.

4. Which coin is worth 25¢?

Ⓐ   Ⓑ   Ⓒ   Ⓓ

5. Which shows the same amount?

Ⓐ

Ⓑ

Ⓒ

Ⓓ

6. Which coins are more than 10¢?

Ⓐ

Ⓑ

Ⓒ

Ⓓ

7. Which coins are more than 25¢?

Ⓐ

Ⓑ

Ⓒ

Ⓓ

8. Which can you buy with this money?

Ⓐ 15¢   Ⓒ 42¢

Ⓑ candy bar 37¢   Ⓓ 39¢

Identify and know the value of coins (penny, nickel, dime, quarter) and show different combinations of coins that equal the same value

What Is It?

Name _____

You can count **even** numbers by **2s**.
Here are some **even** numbers: 2, 4, 6, 8, 10, 12, 14, 16, 18, 20

All other numbers are **odd**.
Here are some odd numbers: 1, 3, 5, 7, 9, 11, 13, 15, 17, 19

Color the **even** numbers brown. Color the **odd** numbers blue.

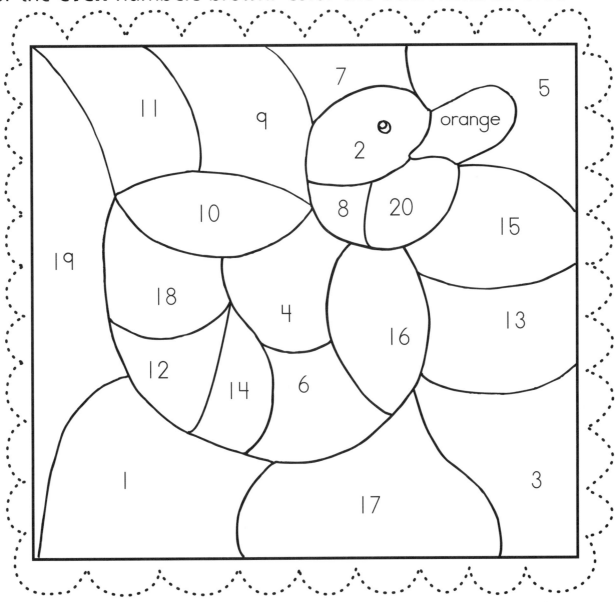

Circle the bird you made.

Identify odd and even numbers

©2003 by Evan-Moor Corp. • Basic Math Skills, Grade 1 • EMC 3014

Number & Operations

Race for the Cheese

Name _____

Circle the **even** numbers.

1	(2)	3	(4)	5	6	7	8	9	10
11	12	13	14	15	16	17	18	19	20

Help the mouse find the cheese. Color the boxes with **even** numbers.

2	6	1	9
5	8	4	7
19	15	12	13
3	16	18	9
17	10	11	5
19	14	20	

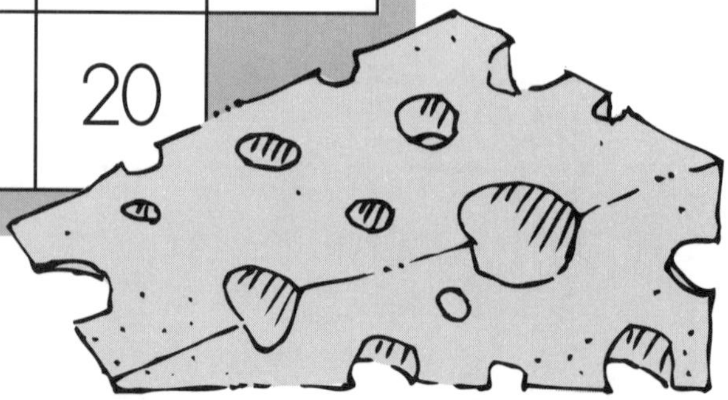

Identify odd and even numbers

Number & Operations

EMC 3014 • Basic Math Skills, Grade 1 • ©2003 by Evan-Moor Corp.

One Left Over

none left over
even

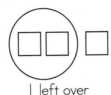
I left over
odd

Is the number of toys even or odd? Circle two at a time.
Then write **even** or **odd**.

1.
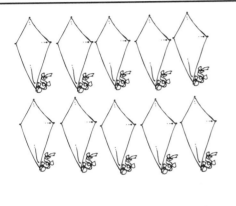
_____

2.
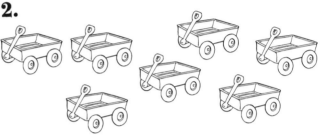
_____

3.
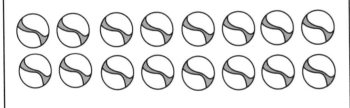
_____

4.

_____

5.

_____

6.
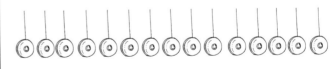
_____

Identify odd and even numbers

Number & Operations

Odd and Even Numbers

Name _____

Circle the **even** numbers. Draw a box around the **odd** numbers.

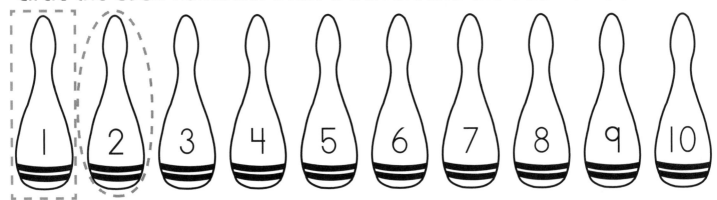

Count the pins that are knocked down. Circle **odd** or **even**.

1.

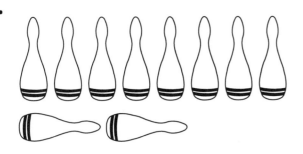

___2___ knocked down

odd (even)

2.

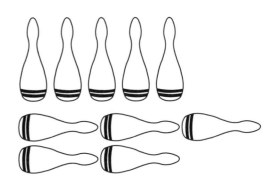

_____ knocked down

odd   even

3.

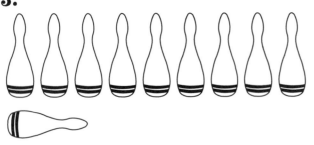

_____ knocked down

odd   even

4.

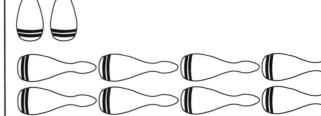

_____ knocked down

odd   even

Identify odd and even numbers

EMC 3014 • Basic Math Skills, Grade 1 • ©2003 by Evan-Moor Corp.

Pick a Team

Who is on each team? Write the names.

★ Jamal's Team ★ (**odd** numbers)	★ Kim's Team ★ (**even** numbers)
_____	_____
_____	_____
_____	_____
_____	_____
_____	_____

Identify odd and even numbers

Number & Operations

Math Test

Fill in the circle next to the correct answer.

1. Find the even number of balls.

Ⓐ 🎾🎾

Ⓑ 🎾🎾 🎾🎾 🎾🎾

Ⓒ 🎾🎾 🎾

Ⓓ 🎾🎾 🎾🎾 🎾🎾 🎾

2. Find the odd number of balls.

Ⓐ 🎾🎾 🎾🎾

Ⓑ 🎾🎾 🎾🎾 🎾

Ⓒ 🎾🎾

Ⓓ 🎾🎾 🎾🎾 🎾🎾

3. Which number is even?
Ⓐ 3
Ⓑ 6
Ⓒ 9
Ⓓ 11

4. Which number is odd?
Ⓐ 14
Ⓑ 16
Ⓒ 15
Ⓓ 10

5. What number comes next in this pattern?

1, 3, 5, _____

Ⓐ 6
Ⓑ 9
Ⓒ 7
Ⓓ 4

6. What number comes next in this pattern?

6, 8, 10, _____

Ⓐ 9
Ⓑ 11
Ⓒ 12
Ⓓ 7

7. What number is missing?
16, 18, 20, _____, 24

Ⓐ 21   Ⓒ 22
Ⓑ 23   Ⓓ 19

8. Put these numbers in order.
11, 7, 3, 5, 9

Ⓐ 11, 9, 7, 3, 5
Ⓑ 7, 9, 11, 5, 3
Ⓒ 3, 7, 9, 5, 11
Ⓓ 3, 5, 7, 9, 11

Identify odd and even numbers

Finish the
Ice-Cream Cone

Read the counting words. Connect the dots in order.

first   second   third   fourth   fifth   sixth   seventh   eighth   ninth   tenth

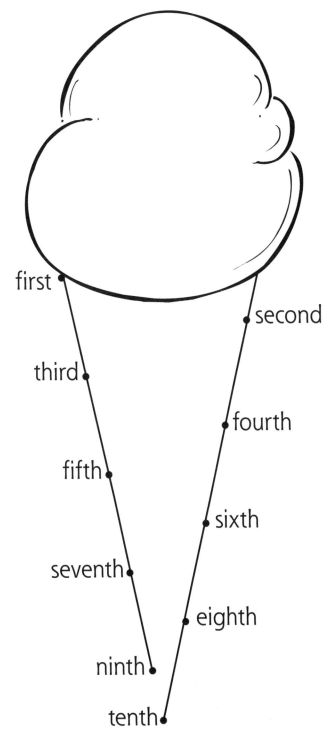

Use ordinal numbers to sequence objects

The Winners

Name _____

Look at the winners of the spelling bee. Put their names in order.

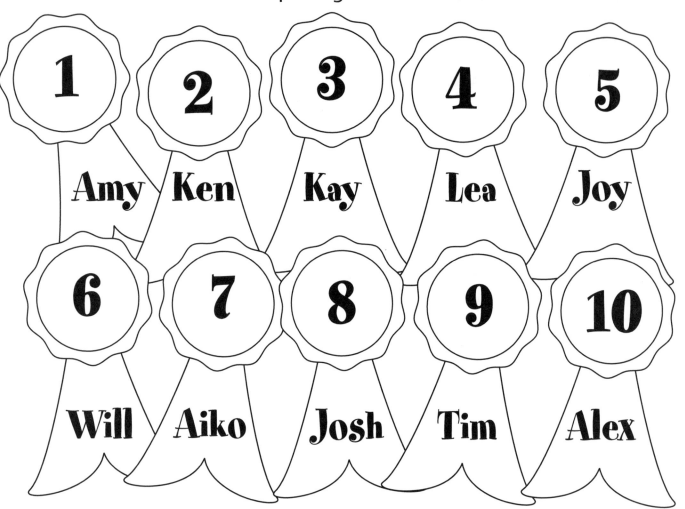

1 Amy   2 Ken   3 Kay   4 Lea   5 Joy

6 Will   7 Aiko   8 Josh   9 Tim   10 Alex

Write each student's name on the correct line.

first _____Amy_____   fifth _____

sixth _____   seventh _____

third _____   second _____

fourth _____   ninth _____

eighth _____   tenth _____

Use ordinal numbers to sequence objects

Bake a Birthday Cake

Help Mom make a cake. Cut out the pictures and paste them in order.
Write the number words under the boxes to tell Mom what to do
first, **second**, **third**, **fourth**, **fifth**, and **sixth**.

first

Use ordinal numbers to sequence objects

Number & Operations

On the Farm

Name _____

first	second	third	fourth	fifth	sixth	seventh	eighth
1st	2nd	3rd	4th	5th	6th	7th	8th

Circle the answer.

1. Who is first?

2. Who is last?

3. Who is between the 4th and 6th animal?

Write the order.

4. The is _____ in line.

5. The  is _____ in line.

6. The is _____ in line.

7. The is _____ in line.

Mama duck had babies!
Make an **X** on the 3rd baby duck. Circle the 5th baby duck.

Use ordinal numbers to sequence objects

  EMC 3014 • Basic Math Skills, Grade 1 • ©2003 by Evan-Moor Corp.

Cats in a Row

I colored the second cat yellow.

Color any three of the cats. Use different colors.

Now tell about the three cats you colored.
Use number words like **first** and **tenth**.

1. _____

   _____

2. _____

   _____

3. _____

   _____

Use ordinal numbers to sequence objects

Name _____

Fill in the circle next to the correct answer.

1. Who is second?

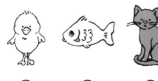

ⓐ   ⓑ   © 　 ⓓ

2. Who is fourth?

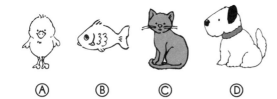

ⓐ   ⓑ   © 　 ⓓ

3. Where is the bird?

ⓐ first
ⓑ second
© third
ⓓ fourth

4. Who is fifth?

Bob   Jill   Ann   Tom   Raul   Ken

ⓐ Tom
ⓑ Raul
© Ken
ⓓ Jill

5. Where is Ken?

Bob   Jill   Ann   Tom   Raul   Ken

ⓐ first
ⓑ third
© fourth
ⓓ sixth

6. Find the ninth dot.

ⓐ   ⓑ   ©   ⓓ

7. Find the third dot.

ⓐ   ⓑ   ©   ⓓ

8. Find the seventh dot.

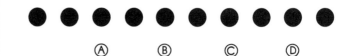

ⓐ   ⓑ   ©   ⓓ

Use ordinal numbers to sequence objects

82   **Number & Operations**   EMC 3014 • Basic Math Skills, Grade 1 • ©2003 by Evan-Moor Corp.

Catching Polliwogs

Name _____

Hector wants to catch polliwogs. Show him how to get to the pond.
Connect the shapes that show $\frac{1}{2}$.

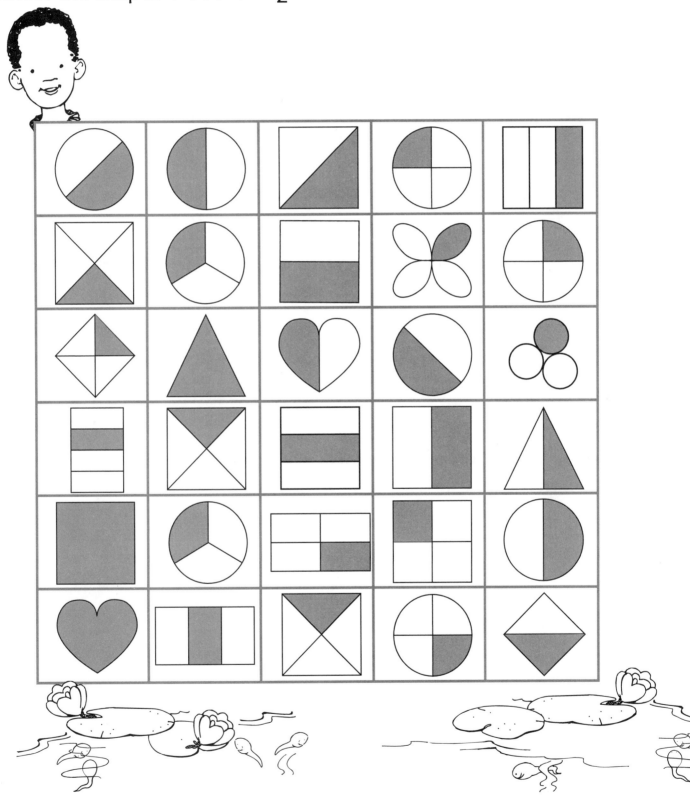

Read, write, and draw fractions (1/2, 1/3, 1/4)

Number & Operations

More Than One Way

Name _____

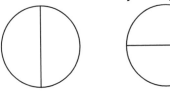

halves = **2** equal parts

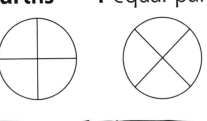

fourths = **4** equal parts

1. Draw lines. Make 2 equal parts for each shape.
   Make each shape different.

2. Draw lines. Make 4 equal parts for each shape.
   Make each shape different.

3. Go back to number 1. Color $\frac{1}{2}$ of each shape.

4. Go back to number 2. Color $\frac{1}{4}$ of each shape.

Read, write, and draw fractions (1/2, 1/3, 1/4)

Number & Operations   EMC 3014 • Basic Math Skills, Grade 1 • ©2003 by Evan-Moor Corp.

Name the Fraction

Name _____

1 $\frac{1}{2}$ $\frac{1}{2}$ $\frac{1}{3}$ $\frac{1}{3}$ $\frac{1}{3}$ $\frac{1}{4}$ $\frac{1}{4}$ $\frac{1}{4}$ $\frac{1}{4}$

Circle the correct fraction.

1.
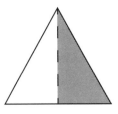

$\frac{1}{2}$ $\frac{1}{4}$ $\frac{1}{3}$

2.

$\frac{1}{2}$ $\frac{1}{4}$ $\frac{1}{3}$

3.
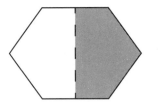

$\frac{1}{2}$ $\frac{1}{4}$ $\frac{1}{3}$

4.

$\frac{1}{2}$ $\frac{1}{4}$ $\frac{1}{3}$

5.

$\frac{1}{2}$ $\frac{1}{4}$ $\frac{1}{3}$

6.
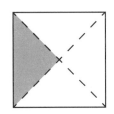

$\frac{1}{2}$ $\frac{1}{4}$ $\frac{1}{3}$

7.
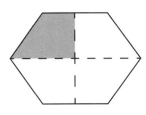

$\frac{1}{2}$ $\frac{1}{4}$ $\frac{1}{3}$

8.

$\frac{1}{2}$ $\frac{1}{4}$ $\frac{1}{3}$

9.
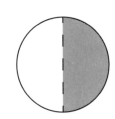

$\frac{1}{2}$ $\frac{1}{4}$ $\frac{1}{3}$

Read, write, and draw fractions (1/2, 1/3, 1/4)

Number & Operations

Fractions of Food

Name _____

1. Circle each food that shows $\frac{1}{2}$ shaded.

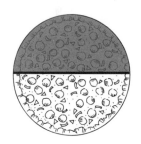 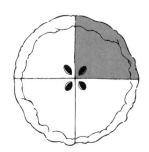 

2. Circle each food that shows $\frac{1}{3}$ shaded.

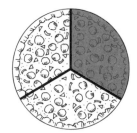 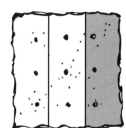 

3. Circle each food that shows $\frac{1}{4}$ shaded.

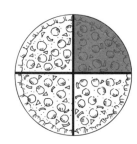 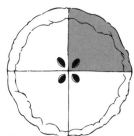 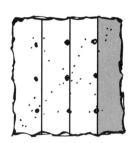

4. How much of this pie is gone? Write $\frac{1}{2}$, $\frac{1}{3}$, or $\frac{1}{4}$.

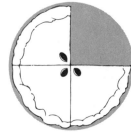 _____ gone

Read, write, and draw fractions (1/2, 1/3, 1/4)

Number & Operations

EMC 3014 • Basic Math Skills, Grade 1 • ©2003 by Evan-Moor Corp.

Sharing Lunch

Name _____

1. Al gave $\frac{1}{2}$ of his sandwich to Jeff. Color the part that Al gave to Jeff.

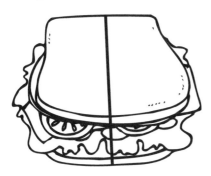

2. Sara gave $\frac{1}{3}$ of her snack to Pat. Color the part that Sara gave to Pat.

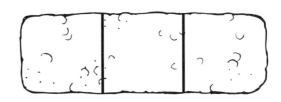

3. Lea gave $\frac{1}{2}$ of her orange to Pete. Color the part that Lea has left.

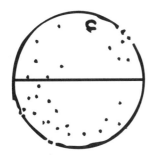

4. Karl gave $\frac{1}{4}$ of his big cookie to Joe and $\frac{1}{4}$ of it to Ann. Color the part that Karl has left.

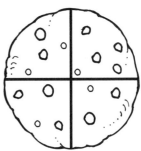

5. Write a word problem about this picture.

_____

_____

_____

_____

Read, write, and draw fractions (1/2, 1/3, 1/4)

Number & Operations

Math Test

Fill in the circle next to the correct answer.

1. Which one shows $\frac{1}{2}$?

   Ⓐ   Ⓑ   Ⓒ   Ⓓ

2. Which one shows $\frac{1}{4}$?

   Ⓐ   Ⓑ   Ⓒ   Ⓓ

3. Which one shows $\frac{1}{3}$?

   Ⓐ   Ⓑ   Ⓒ   Ⓓ

4. How much is colored?

Ⓐ $\frac{1}{4}$ Ⓑ $\frac{1}{3}$ Ⓒ I Ⓓ $\frac{1}{2}$

5. Which one shows thirds?

   Ⓐ   Ⓑ   Ⓒ   Ⓓ

6. Which one shows halves?

   Ⓐ   Ⓑ   Ⓒ   Ⓓ

7. Which one shows fourths?

Ⓐ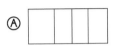

Ⓑ

Ⓒ

Ⓓ

8. Margo gave $\frac{1}{2}$ of her candy bar to Tammy. How much did she give Tammy?

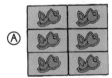

Ⓐ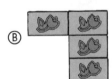

Ⓑ

Ⓒ

Ⓓ

Read, write, and draw fractions (1/2, 1/3, 1/4)

Some for You and Some for Me

Name _____

Color the parts.

for **me**—  red

for **you**— blue

 $\frac{1}{2}$ = 1 of 2

$\frac{1}{3}$ = 1 of 3

 $\frac{1}{4}$ = 1 of 4

1.

$\frac{1}{2}$ for me.

$\frac{1}{2}$ for you.

2.

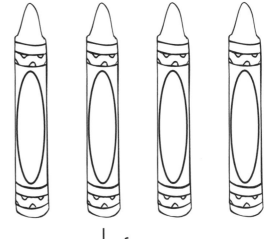

$\frac{1}{4}$ for me.

$\frac{3}{4}$ for you.

3.

$\frac{2}{3}$ for me.

$\frac{1}{3}$ for you.

4.

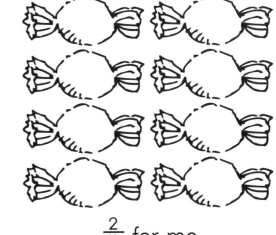

$\frac{2}{4}$ for me.

$\frac{2}{4}$ for you.

Read, write, and draw fractions (1/2, 1/3, 1/4) when given sets of objects

Color the Fractions

Name _____

Color $\frac{1}{2}$ of each group.

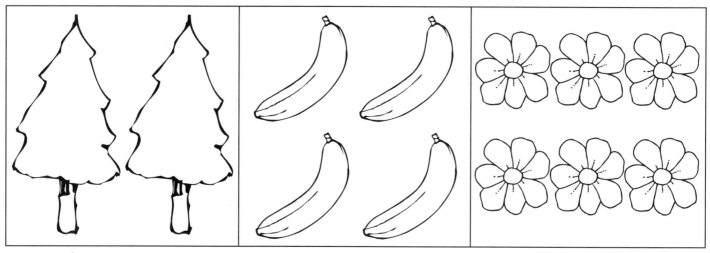

Color $\frac{1}{4}$ of each group.

Color $\frac{1}{3}$ of each group.

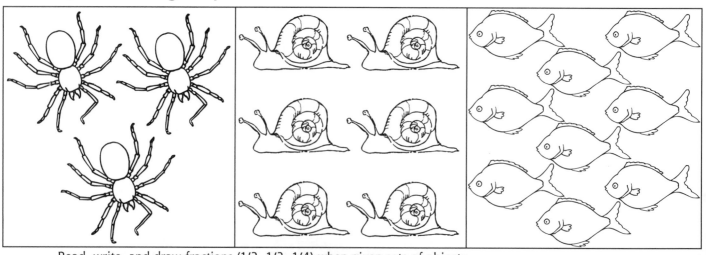

Read, write, and draw fractions (1/2, 1/3, 1/4) when given sets of objects

Number & Operations

Parts of a Group

$\frac{1}{2}$ = 1 of 2

$\frac{1}{3}$ = 1 of 3

$\frac{1}{4}$ = 1 of 4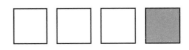

1. Sara has 2 apples.
Circle $\frac{1}{2}$ of Sara's apples.

2. Mark has 4 apples.
Circle $\frac{1}{2}$ of Mark's apples.

3. Dante has 3 cookies.
Circle $\frac{1}{3}$ of Dante's cookies.

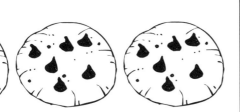

4. Selena has 6 cookies.
Circle $\frac{1}{3}$ of Selena's cookies.

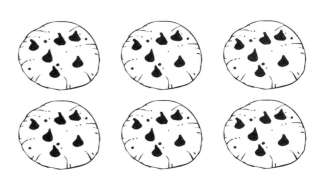

5. Tim has 4 nuts.
Circle $\frac{1}{4}$ of Tim's nuts.

6. Meling has 12 nuts.
Circle $\frac{1}{4}$ of Meling's nuts.

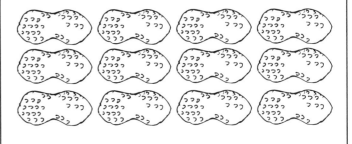

Read, write, and draw fractions (1/2, 1/3, 1/4) when given sets of objects

Number & Operations

Find the Fraction

Name _____

How much is shaded? Circle the number.

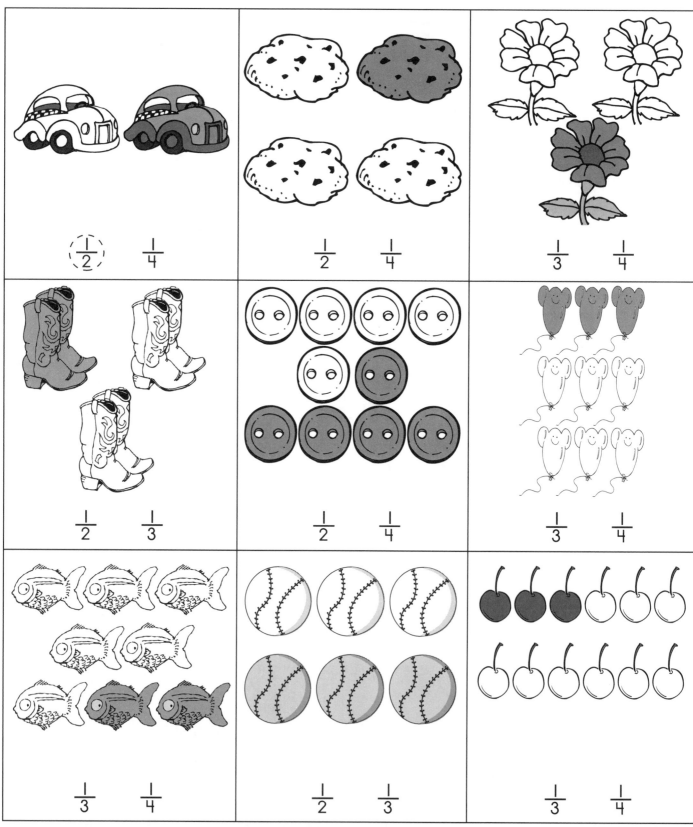

Colorful Flowers

Color the flowers. Follow these steps.

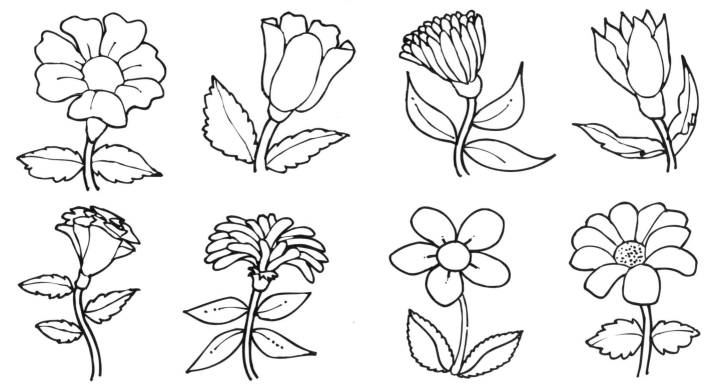

1. Draw a blue box around $\frac{1}{2}$ of the flowers.
   Draw a brown box around the other $\frac{1}{2}$.

2. Go to the blue box.
   Color $\frac{1}{4}$ of the flowers red.
   Draw grass under the other flowers.

3. Go to the brown box.
   Color $\frac{1}{4}$ of the flowers purple.
   Draw grass under the other flowers.

4. Find the flowers with grass in each box.
   Color $\frac{1}{3}$ of those flowers yellow.

5. Color the rest of the flowers any way you want.

Read, write, and draw fractions (1/2, 1/3, 1/4) when given sets of objects

Math Test

Fill in the circle next to the correct answer.

1. Which one shows $\frac{1}{2}$ circled?

Ⓐ

Ⓑ

Ⓒ

Ⓓ

2. Which one shows $\frac{1}{4}$ in a box?

Ⓐ ▣ ● ● ●

Ⓑ ▣ ● ● ●

Ⓒ ● ● ● ●

Ⓓ ● ● ● ●

3. Which one shows $\frac{1}{3}$ circled?

Ⓐ

Ⓑ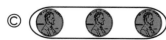

Ⓒ

Ⓓ

4. How much of the group is shaded?

Ⓐ 1   Ⓑ $\frac{1}{2}$ Ⓒ $\frac{1}{3}$ Ⓓ $\frac{1}{4}$

5. How much of the group is shaded?

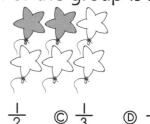

Ⓐ 1   Ⓑ $\frac{1}{2}$ Ⓒ $\frac{1}{3}$ Ⓓ $\frac{1}{4}$

6. Pete had 2 sandwiches. He ate half of them. How many did he eat?

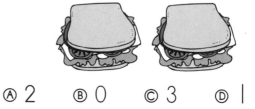

Ⓐ 2   Ⓑ 0   Ⓒ 3   Ⓓ 1

7. Jan's cat had 4 kittens. Jan gave $\frac{1}{4}$ of the kittens to a friend. How many kittens did she give her friend?

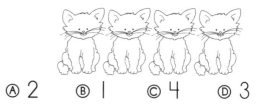

Ⓐ 2   Ⓑ 1   Ⓒ 4   Ⓓ 3

8. Pete had 3 apples. He gave $\frac{1}{3}$ of the apples to his sister. How many did he have left?

Ⓐ 3   Ⓑ 2   Ⓒ 4   Ⓓ 5

Read, write, and draw fractions (1/2, 1/3, 1/4) when given sets of objects

EMC 3014 • Basic Math Skills, Grade 1 • ©2003 by Evan-Moor Corp.

Five in Bed

Name _____

There were 5 in the bed
And the little one said,
"Roll over!"
So the 5 rolled over
And one fell out.

5 – 1 = ____

There were 4 in the bed
And the little one said,
"Roll over!"
So the 4 rolled over
And one fell out.

4 – 1 = ____

There were 3 in the bed
And the little one said,
"Roll over!"
So the 3 rolled over
And one fell out.

3 – 1 = ____

There were 2 in the bed
And the little one said,
"Roll over!"
So the 2 rolled over
And one fell out.

2 – 1 = ____

There was 1 in the bed
And the others said,
"Roll over!"
So the 1 rolled over
And fell out of bed.

1 – 1 = ____

Show the meaning of addition (putting together, increasing) and subtraction (taking away, comparing, finding the difference)

Number & Operations

They Kept Coming!

Name _____

Ann baked cookies.
They smelled so good.
Dan came running
As fast as he could.

$1 + 1 =$ ____

Ann baked cookies.
They smelled so good.
Fran came running
As fast as she could.

$2 + 1 =$ ____

Ann baked cookies.
They smelled so good.
Jan came running
As fast as she could.

$3 + 1 =$ ____

Ann baked cookies.
They smelled so good.
Nan came running
As fast as she could.

$4 + 1 =$ ____

Ann baked cookies.
They smelled so good.
Stan and Van came running
As fast as they could.

$5 + 2 =$ ____

Show the meaning of addition (putting together, increasing) and subtraction (taking away, comparing, finding the difference)

EMC 3014 • Basic Math Skills, Grade 1 • ©2003 by Evan-Moor Corp.

Add and Subtract

Name _____

Find the answers.

1.

___ + ___ = ___

2.

___ − ___ = ___

3.

___ − ___ = ___

4.

___ + ___ = ___

5.

___ − ___ = ___

6.

___ + ___ = ___

7.

___ + ___ = ___

8.

___ − ___ = ___

Draw a picture to help you add or subtract.

5 − 2 = ___	2 + 3 = ___

Show the meaning of addition (putting together, increasing) and subtraction (taking away, comparing, finding the difference)

Six Posies in the Pot

Name _____

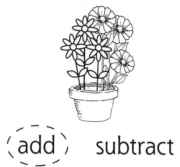

(add)　subtract

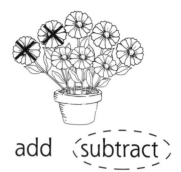

add　(subtract)

Each pot needs 6 posies. Draw more to make 6 or cross out to make 6. Then circle **add** or **subtract**.

1.

add　　subtract

2.

add　　subtract

3.

add　　subtract

4.
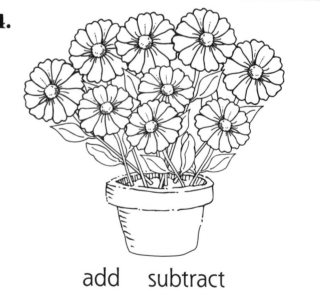

add　　subtract

Show the meaning of addition (putting together, increasing) and subtraction (taking away, comparing, finding the difference)

Number & Operations

EMC 3014 • Basic Math Skills, Grade 1 • ©2003 by Evan-Moor Corp.

Help Hannah

Help Hannah finish her math.
Write the answer.

Name _____

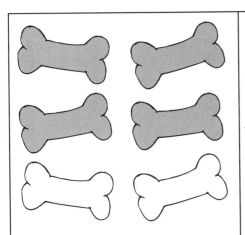

$$2 + 4 = \underline{}$$

$$3 - 2 = \underline{}$$

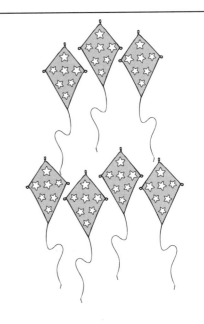

$$7 - 3 = \underline{}$$

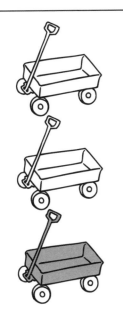

$$2 + 1 = \underline{}$$

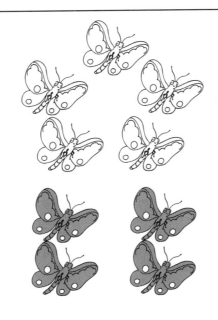

$$5 + 4 = \underline{}$$

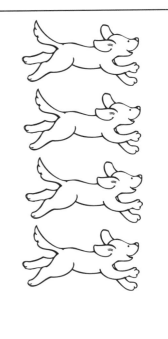

$$4 - 1 = \underline{}$$

Show the meaning of addition (putting together, increasing) and subtraction (taking away, comparing, finding the difference)

Number & Operations

Name _____

Math Test

Fill in the circle next to the correct answer.

1. Which one shows addition?

Ⓐ

Ⓑ

Ⓒ

Ⓓ

2. Which one shows subtraction?

Ⓐ

Ⓑ

Ⓒ

Ⓓ

3. Find the subtraction problem.

Ⓐ 9 – 4
Ⓑ 12 + 7
Ⓒ 8 = 8
Ⓓ 3 + 5

4. Find the addition problem.

Ⓐ 11 – 6
Ⓑ 13 – 6
Ⓒ 9 + 8
Ⓓ 22 – 20

5. Which sign tells you to add?

Ⓐ =
Ⓑ –
Ⓒ +

6. Which sign tells you to subtract?

Ⓐ =
Ⓑ –
Ⓒ +

7. Which sign should you use for this problem?

Amy had 7 cookies. She gave 3 to her friend. How many were left?

Ⓐ =   Ⓑ –   Ⓒ +

8. Which sign should you use for this problem?

Sam picked 3 apples. Eli picked 8 oranges. How many pieces of fruit did they pick?

Ⓐ =   Ⓑ –   Ⓒ +

Show the meaning of addition (putting together, increasing) and subtraction (taking away, comparing, finding the difference)

EMC 3014 • Basic Math Skills, Grade 1 • ©2003 by Evan-Moor Corp.

Riddle

What is black and yellow and buzzes?

Code		
b–0	e–1	h–2
n–3	o–4	y–5

Use the code to solve the riddle.
Write the matching letter below each answer.

5 − 3	2 + 2	4 − 1	1 + 0	3 + 2	4 − 4	5 − 4	1 − 0
□	□	□	□	□	□	□	□

Draw the answer here.

Know the addition facts (sums to 5) and the corresponding subtraction facts and commit them to memory

Number & Operations

Blowing Bubbles

Name _____

Add or subtract. Find the answers. Color the bubbles.

Key

0–green   1–yellow   2–red
3–blue   4–orange   5–purple

Know the addition facts (sums to 5) and the corresponding subtraction facts and commit them to memory

EMC 3014 • Basic Math Skills, Grade 1 • ©2003 by Evan-Moor Corp.

Hungry Caterpillars

Name _____

Find the answers. Draw a line from each to the with the correct answer.

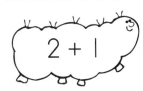 2 + 1

 0

 5 - 3

 5 - 5

 1

 3 + 2

 2

 2 + 3

 4 - 3

 3

 3 - 3

 2 + 2

 4

5

1 + 0

Draw a picture to show each number sentence. Write the answer.

2 + 1 = ____	4 - 2 = ____	3 + 2 = ____

Know the addition facts (sums to 5) and the corresponding subtraction facts and commit them to memory

Do I Belong?

1. Make an **X** on the problems that do NOT equal **1.**

0 + 1	1 – 0	1 – 1	2 + 1
5 – 4	4 – 3	3 – 2	2 – 1

2. Make an **X** on the problems that do NOT equal **2.**

1 + 1	2 + 0	2 – 0	3 + 1
4 – 2	3 – 1	1 – 1	5 – 3

3. Make an **X** on the problems that do NOT equal **3.**

3 + 0	4 + 1	2 + 1	3 – 3
1 + 2	3 – 0	4 – 1	5 – 2

4. Make an **X** on the problems that do NOT equal **4.**

2 + 2	3 + 1	1 + 3	4 – 0
2 + 3	5 – 1	2 – 2	4 + 1

Know the addition facts (sums to 5) and the corresponding subtraction facts and commit them to memory

Number & Operations

EMC 3014 • Basic Math Skills, Grade 1 • ©2003 by Evan-Moor Corp.

Fruit Trees

Draw pictures to help you solve these problems.

1. Lisa picked 2 🟠 from one tree. She picked 3 🟠 from another tree. How many 🟠 did she pick?

_____ oranges

2. Ben had 3 🍒. He ate 1 of them. How many 🍒 did he have left?

_____ cherries

3. There were 5 🍋 on a tree. Dalia picked 3 of them. How many 🍋 were left on the tree?

_____ lemons

4. Joey had 2 red 🍎 and 1 green 🍏. How many 🍎 did he have in all?

_____ apples

5. A 🐿 ate 3 🌰 from the tree. Then it ate 2 more. How many 🌰 did it eat?

_____ nuts

6. Jesse picked 2 🧺. His sister picked 2 🧺. How many 🧺 did they pick?

_____ baskets

7. Write a word problem about this picture.

_____

_____

_____

_____

Know the addition facts (sums to 5) and the corresponding subtraction facts and commit them to memory

Name _____

Fill in the circle next to the correct answer.

1. 2 + 2 = _____
   Ⓐ 2   Ⓑ 4   Ⓒ 3   Ⓓ 5

2. 5 − 3 = _____
   Ⓐ 1   Ⓑ 3   Ⓒ 0   Ⓓ 2

3. Which problem equals 5?
   Ⓐ 5 − 4
   Ⓑ 1 + 3
   Ⓒ 3 + 2
   Ⓓ 4 − 0

4. Which problem has the same sum as 3 + 1?
   Ⓐ 5 − 1
   Ⓑ 3 + 2
   Ⓒ 4 − 1
   Ⓓ 2 + 3

5. Which number sentence is NOT correct?
   Ⓐ 4 − 0 = 4
   Ⓑ 5 + 0 = 5
   Ⓒ 4 − 0 = 0
   Ⓓ 5 − 0 = 5

6. There are 3 ants on a log. Then 1 more ant joins them. How many ants are on the log?
   Ⓐ 3
   Ⓑ 4
   Ⓒ 5
   Ⓓ 1

7. There are 5 butterflies on a plant. Then 2 butterflies fly away. How many are left?
   Ⓐ 6 butterflies
   Ⓑ 2 butterflies
   Ⓒ 3 butterflies
   Ⓓ 4 butterflies

8. Which number sentence tells about this picture?

   Ⓐ 5 + 0 = 5
   Ⓑ 5 − 2 = 3
   Ⓒ 5 − 3 = 2
   Ⓓ 5 + 3 = 2

Know the addition facts (sums to 5) and the corresponding subtraction facts and commit them to memory

A Colorful Toucan

Name _____

Find the answers. Color the picture.

$$10 - 2$$

$$3 + 6$$

$$5 + 3$$

$$9 + 0 =$$

$$3 + 3$$

$$9 - 4 =$$

$$10 - 1$$

$$4 + 2 =$$

$$4 + 6$$

$$10 - 2$$

$$5 + 4$$

$$9 - 1$$

$$8 + 0 =$$

$$1 + 9 =$$

$$8 - 2$$

$$3 + 3$$

$$10 - 3 =$$

$$5 + 2 =$$

$$7 + 3 =$$

$$10 - 1$$

$$4 + 4$$

Key

10–red
9–green
8–blue
7–brown
6–orange
5–black

Know the addition facts (sums to 10) and the corresponding subtraction facts and commit them to memory

A Corny Riddle!

Name _____

Use the code to solve the riddle. Write the matching letter below each answer.

Key	
1–a	6–v
2–l	7–r
3–e	8–s
4–h	9–t
5–p	10–n

Why can't you tell secrets in a cornfield?

5 +4	8 –4	3 +0

9 –4	10 –8	6 –5	5 +5	10 –1	5 +3

___ ___ ___   ___ ___ ___ ___ ___ ___

8 –4	7 –6	9 –3	2 +1

9 –6	10 –9	3 +4	10 –2

___ ___ ___ ___   ___ ___ ___ ___

Know the addition facts (sums to 10) and the corresponding subtraction facts and commit them to memory

EMC 3014 • Basic Math Skills, Grade 1 • ©2003 by Evan-Moor Corp.

Let's Make 10

Name _____

Use the bugs to help you find the missing numbers.

___ + ___ = 10   ___ + ___ = 10

___ + ___ = 10   ___ + ___ = 10

___ + ___ = 10   ___ + ___ = 10

___ + ___ = 10   ___ + ___ = 10

___ + ___ = 10   ___ + ___ = 10

Find the answers. Circle the problems that equal **10**.

8	9	4	7	4	10	3	6
$-\,1$	$-\,5$	$+\,6$	$-\,2$	$-\,1$	$-\,8$	$+\,5$	$-\,4$

3	9	7	8	10	6	5	5
$+\,6$	$+\,1$	$+\,2$	$-\,5$	$-\,5$	$+\,3$	$+\,4$	$+\,5$

7	3	3	9	10	8	2	7
$-\,3$	$+\,4$	$+\,3$	$-\,2$	$-\,4$	$+\,2$	$+\,5$	$+\,3$

Know the addition facts (sums to 10) and the corresponding subtraction facts and commit them to memory

Make a Match

Name _____

Match each problem to its answer.

3 + 5	10	5 + 4	9
7 + 3	8	9 – 2	5
8 – 2	3	8 + 2	7
3 – 0	6	7 – 2	10
3 + 4	3	6 + 4	6
1 + 7	7	9 – 1	8
9 – 6	10	6 + 3	9
10 – 0	8	10 – 4	10

Know the addition facts (sums to 10) and the corresponding subtraction facts and commit them to memory

Number & Operations

EMC 3014 • Basic Math Skills, Grade 1 • ©2003 by Evan-Moor Corp.

A Flock of Birds

Name _____

1. There are 5 birds in a tree.
Then 3 birds fly away.
How many birds are left?

_____ ◯ _____ = _____

2. There are 6 birds on the ground.
Then 4 more birds come.
How many birds are there in all?

_____ ◯ _____ = _____

3. There are 8 black birds and
4 green birds in a tree.
How many more black birds
than green birds are there?

_____ ◯ _____ = _____

4. Write a word problem about this picture.
Then write the number sentence about it.

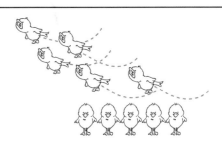

_____ ◯ _____ = _____

_____

_____

_____

Know the addition facts (sums to 10) and the corresponding subtraction facts and commit them to memory

Name _____

Fill in the circle next to the correct answer.

1. 3 + 3 = _____
- Ⓐ 6
- Ⓑ 8
- Ⓒ 0
- Ⓓ 4

2. 8 + 2 = _____
- Ⓐ 6
- Ⓑ 9
- Ⓒ 10
- Ⓓ 4

3. 9 − 3 = _____
- Ⓐ 7
- Ⓑ 5
- Ⓒ 10
- Ⓓ 6

4. 5 − 5 = _____
- Ⓐ 10
- Ⓑ 5
- Ⓒ 0
- Ⓓ 8

5. Which problem has the same sum as 3 + 7?
- Ⓐ 0 + 9
- Ⓑ 3 + 4
- Ⓒ 7 + 2
- Ⓓ 10 + 0

6. Which number sentence is NOT correct?
- Ⓐ 5 + 4 = 9
- Ⓑ 9 − 4 = 5
- Ⓒ 9 + 5 = 4
- Ⓓ 4 + 5 = 9

7. A big bird ate 10 worms. A small bird ate 6 worms. How many more worms did the big bird eat?
- Ⓐ 9
- Ⓑ 3
- Ⓒ 1
- Ⓓ 4

8. Find the number sentence for this picture.

- Ⓐ 6 − 3 = 3
- Ⓑ 6 + 3 = 9
- Ⓒ 9 − 3 = 6
- Ⓓ 3 + 3 = 6

Know the addition facts (sums to 10) and the corresponding subtraction facts and commit them to memory

  EMC 3014 • Basic Math Skills, Grade 1 • ©2003 by Evan-Moor Corp.

A House of Facts

Name _____

Finish the house for each fact family. Write the answers.
Then cut and paste.

$3 + 6 =$ ___

$9 - 6 =$ ___

$8 + 2 =$ ___

$10 - 2 =$ ___

$4 + 3 =$ ___

$7 - 3 =$ ___

$7 + 3 =$ ___

$10 - 3 =$ ___

$6 + 3 =$ ___

$9 - 3 =$ ___

$3 + 4 =$ ___

$7 - 4 =$ ___

$2 + 8 =$ ___

$10 - 8 =$ ___

$3 + 7 =$ ___

$10 - 7 =$ ___

Use the inverse relationship between addition and subtraction to solve problems

Number & Operations

Up the Mountain and Down Again

Add your way up the mountain. Subtract your way down.
Draw a line between the problems with the same numbers.

$5 + 5 = \boxed{}$ $10 - 5 = \boxed{}$

$4 + 2 = \boxed{}$ $6 - 2 = \boxed{}$

$3 + 7 = \boxed{}$ $10 - 7 = \boxed{}$

$6 + 2 = \boxed{}$ $8 - 2 = \boxed{}$

$2 + 4 = \boxed{}$ $6 - 4 = \boxed{}$

$1 + 6 = \boxed{}$ $7 - 6 = \boxed{}$

$7 + 2 = \boxed{}$ $9 - 2 = \boxed{}$

$6 + 4 = \boxed{}$ $10 - 4 = \boxed{}$

$4 + 1 = \boxed{}$ $5 - 1 = \boxed{}$

Use the inverse relationship between addition and subtraction to solve problems

Check the Answers

Check subtraction by adding.

Name _____

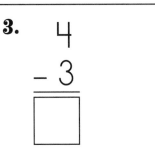
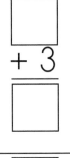

1.
$$\begin{array}{r} 6 \\ -\ 2 \\ \hline \boxed{4} \end{array}$$

$$\begin{array}{r} \boxed{4} \\ +\ 2 \\ \hline \boxed{} \end{array}$$

2.
$$\begin{array}{r} 9 \\ -\ 6 \\ \hline \boxed{} \end{array}$$

$$\begin{array}{r} \boxed{} \\ +\ 6 \\ \hline \boxed{} \end{array}$$

3.
$$\begin{array}{r} 4 \\ -\ 3 \\ \hline \boxed{} \end{array}$$

$$\begin{array}{r} \boxed{} \\ +\ 3 \\ \hline \boxed{} \end{array}$$

4.
$$\begin{array}{r} 7 \\ -\ 4 \\ \hline \boxed{} \end{array}$$

$$\begin{array}{r} \boxed{} \\ +\ 4 \\ \hline \boxed{} \end{array}$$

5.
$$\begin{array}{r} 9 \\ -\ 9 \\ \hline \boxed{} \end{array}$$

$$\begin{array}{r} \boxed{} \\ +\ 9 \\ \hline \boxed{} \end{array}$$

6.
$$\begin{array}{r} 10 \\ -\ 7 \\ \hline \boxed{} \end{array}$$

$$\begin{array}{r} \boxed{} \\ +\ 7 \\ \hline \boxed{} \end{array}$$

7.
$$\begin{array}{r} 6 \\ -\ 4 \\ \hline \boxed{} \end{array}$$

$$\begin{array}{r} \boxed{} \\ +\ 4 \\ \hline \boxed{} \end{array}$$

8.
$$\begin{array}{r} 9 \\ -\ 3 \\ \hline \boxed{} \end{array}$$

$$\begin{array}{r} \boxed{} \\ +\ 3 \\ \hline \boxed{} \end{array}$$

9.
$$\begin{array}{r} 8 \\ -\ 6 \\ \hline \boxed{} \end{array}$$

$$\begin{array}{r} \boxed{} \\ +\ 6 \\ \hline \boxed{} \end{array}$$

10.
$$\begin{array}{r} 7 \\ -\ 2 \\ \hline \boxed{} \end{array}$$

$$\begin{array}{r} \boxed{} \\ +\ 2 \\ \hline \boxed{} \end{array}$$

11.
$$\begin{array}{r} 10 \\ -\ 3 \\ \hline \boxed{} \end{array}$$

$$\begin{array}{r} \boxed{} \\ +\ 3 \\ \hline \boxed{} \end{array}$$

12.
$$\begin{array}{r} 6 \\ -\ 6 \\ \hline \boxed{} \end{array}$$

$$\begin{array}{r} \boxed{} \\ +\ 6 \\ \hline \boxed{} \end{array}$$

13.
$$\begin{array}{r} 8 \\ -\ 2 \\ \hline \boxed{} \end{array}$$

$$\begin{array}{r} \boxed{} \\ +\ 2 \\ \hline \boxed{} \end{array}$$

14.
$$\begin{array}{r} 10 \\ -\ 8 \\ \hline \boxed{} \end{array}$$

$$\begin{array}{r} \boxed{} \\ +\ 8 \\ \hline \boxed{} \end{array}$$

15.
$$\begin{array}{r} 7 \\ -\ 1 \\ \hline \boxed{} \end{array}$$

$$\begin{array}{r} \boxed{} \\ +\ 1 \\ \hline \boxed{} \end{array}$$

Use the inverse relationship between addition and subtraction to solve problems

Number & Operations

Fact Families

Use the numbers to make fact families.

5 2 7

___ + ___ = ___

___ + ___ = ___

___ − ___ = ___

___ − ___ = ___

6 4 10

___ + ___ = ___

___ + ___ = ___

___ − ___ = ___

___ − ___ = ___

8 1 9

___ + ___ = ___

___ + ___ = ___

___ − ___ = ___

___ − ___ = ___

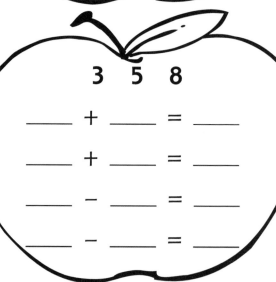

3 5 8

___ + ___ = ___

___ + ___ = ___

___ − ___ = ___

___ − ___ = ___

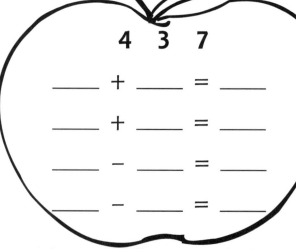

4 3 7

___ + ___ = ___

___ + ___ = ___

___ − ___ = ___

___ − ___ = ___

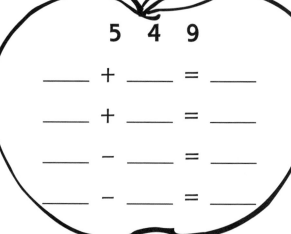

5 4 9

___ + ___ = ___

___ + ___ = ___

___ − ___ = ___

___ − ___ = ___

Use the inverse relationship between addition and subtraction to solve problems

EMC 3014 • Basic Math Skills, Grade 1 • ©2003 by Evan-Moor Corp.

Use What You Know

I know 6 + 3 is 9, so 9 – 6 must be 3.

9 + 6 = 15   so   15 – 9 = __6__

2 + 5 = 7   so   7 – 2 = ____

4 + 6 = 10   so   10 – 4 = ____

5 + 3 = 8   so   8 – 5 = ____

3 + 4 = 7   so   7 – 3 = ____

2 + 5 = 7   so   7 – 2 = ____

4 + 5 = 9   so   9 – 4 = ____

3 + 6 = 9   so   9 – 3 = ____

2 + 6 = 8   so   8 – 2 = ____

4 + 2 = 6   so   6 – 4 = ____

10 – 9 = 1   so   9 + 1 = __10__

8 – 3 = 5   so   3 + 5 = ____

10 – 4 = 6   so   4 + 6 = ____

8 – 4 = 4   so   4 + 4 = ____

9 – 3 = 6   so   3 + 6 = ____

7 – 2 = 5   so   2 + 5 = ____

9 – 4 = 5   so   4 + 5 = ____

8 – 2 = 6   so   2 + 6 = ____

10 – 5 = 5   so   5 + 5 = ____

10 – 3 = 7   so   3 + 7 = ____

Use the inverse relationship between addition and subtraction to solve problems

Number & Operations

Math Test

Fill in the circle next to the correct answer.

1. $2 + 7 = 9$ so $9 - 2 = $ _____
  Ⓐ 2
  Ⓑ 9
  Ⓒ 7
  Ⓓ 11

2. $3 - 2 = 1$ so $1 + 2 = $ _____
  Ⓐ 5
  Ⓑ 2
  Ⓒ 1
  Ⓓ 3

3. $9 + 1 = 10$ so $10 - 9 = $ _____
  Ⓐ 1
  Ⓑ 2
  Ⓒ 3
  Ⓓ 0

4. $10 - 2 = 8$ so $2 + 8 = $ _____
  Ⓐ 4
  Ⓑ 10
  Ⓒ 8
  Ⓓ 0

5. Which number sentence can you make with these numbers?
       2, 5, 7
  Ⓐ $7 + 2 = 5$ Ⓒ $5 - 2 = 3$
  Ⓑ $7 - 5 = 2$ Ⓓ $7 - 3 = 5$

6. What numbers are in this fact family?
       $2 + 8 = 10$ $10 - 2 = 8$
       $8 + 2 = 10$ $10 - 8 = 2$
  Ⓐ 8, 10, 0
  Ⓑ 10, 2, 6
  Ⓒ 4, 6, 10
  Ⓓ 2, 8, 10

7. Which number sentence is NOT part of the same fact family?
  Ⓐ $4 - 1 = 3$
  Ⓑ $1 + 3 = 4$
  Ⓒ $4 - 4 = 0$
  Ⓓ $4 - 3 = 1$

8. Which number sentence is NOT part of the same fact family?
  Ⓐ $6 + 2 = 8$
  Ⓑ $8 - 2 = 6$
  Ⓒ $8 - 6 = 2$
  Ⓓ $8 - 3 = 5$

Use the inverse relationship between addition and subtraction to solve problems

Park the Car

Start

$$\begin{array}{r} 9 \\ + 4 \\ \hline \end{array}$$
$$\begin{array}{r} 12 \\ - 3 \\ \hline \end{array}$$
$$\begin{array}{r} 5 \\ + 8 \\ \hline \end{array}$$
$$\begin{array}{r} 11 \\ - 3 \\ \hline \end{array}$$
$$\begin{array}{r} 10 \\ + 2 \\ \hline \end{array}$$

$$\begin{array}{r} 13 \\ - 9 \\ \hline \end{array}$$

$$\begin{array}{r} 8 \\ + 4 \\ \hline \end{array}$$
$$\begin{array}{r} 12 \\ - 6 \\ \hline \end{array}$$
$$\begin{array}{r} 11 \\ - 5 \\ \hline \end{array}$$
$$\begin{array}{r} 12 \\ - 9 \\ \hline \end{array}$$
$$\begin{array}{r} 7 \\ + 4 \\ \hline \end{array}$$
$$\begin{array}{r} 10 \\ + 3 \\ \hline \end{array}$$

$$\begin{array}{r} 3 \\ + 8 \\ \hline \end{array}$$

$$\begin{array}{r} 11 \\ - 1 \\ \hline \end{array}$$

$$\begin{array}{r} 9 \\ + 3 \\ \hline \end{array}$$
$$\begin{array}{r} 13 \\ - 6 \\ \hline \end{array}$$
$$\begin{array}{r} 12 \\ - 8 \\ \hline \end{array}$$
$$\begin{array}{r} 5 \\ + 7 \\ \hline \end{array}$$
$$\begin{array}{r} 13 \\ - 3 \\ \hline \end{array}$$
$$\begin{array}{r} 6 \\ + 5 \\ \hline \end{array}$$

Know the addition facts (sums to 13) and the corresponding subtraction facts and commit them to memory

Mother Hen

Name _____

Add or subtract. Find the color for each answer. Color the picture.

Key

8–orange   11–yellow
9–blue   12–green
10–red   13–brown

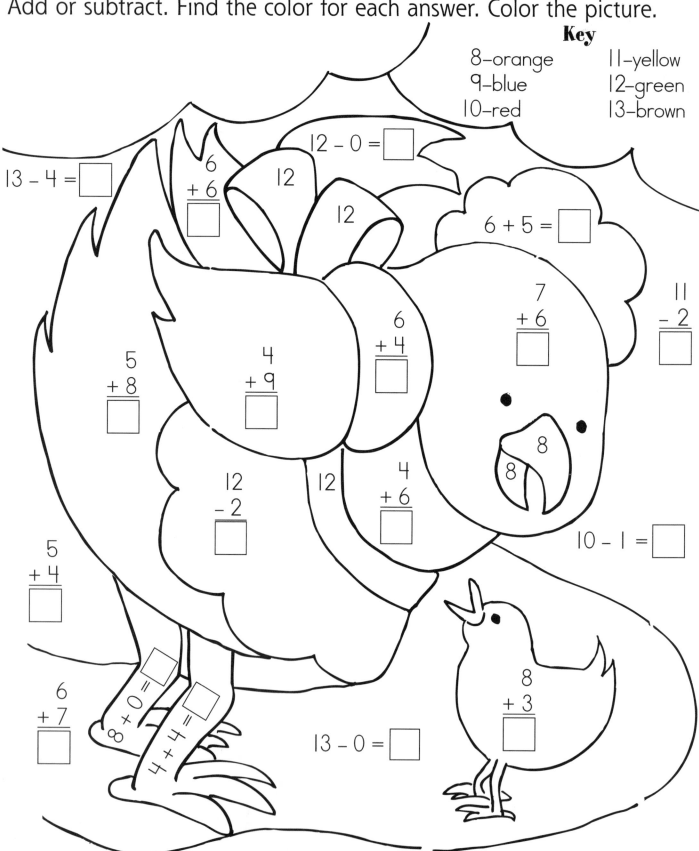

Know the addition facts (sums to 13) and the corresponding subtraction facts and commit them to memory

EMC 3014 • Basic Math Skills, Grade 1 • ©2003 by Evan-Moor Corp.

Ant Antics

Use the ants to help you solve these problems.

1.
$$\begin{array}{r} 9 \\ + 3 \\ \hline 12 \end{array}$$
$$\begin{array}{r} 12 \\ - 9 \\ \hline \end{array}$$
$$\begin{array}{r} 11 \\ - 4 \\ \hline \end{array}$$
$$\begin{array}{r} 10 \\ + 3 \\ \hline \end{array}$$
$$\begin{array}{r} 5 \\ + 8 \\ \hline \end{array}$$
$$\begin{array}{r} 13 \\ - 8 \\ \hline \end{array}$$

2.
$$\begin{array}{r} 11 \\ - 2 \\ \hline \end{array}$$
$$\begin{array}{r} 12 \\ - 7 \\ \hline \end{array}$$
$$\begin{array}{r} 5 \\ + 6 \\ \hline \end{array}$$
$$\begin{array}{r} 11 \\ - 7 \\ \hline \end{array}$$
$$\begin{array}{r} 4 \\ + 7 \\ \hline \end{array}$$
$$\begin{array}{r} 9 \\ + 4 \\ \hline \end{array}$$

3.
$$\begin{array}{r} 13 \\ - 7 \\ \hline \end{array}$$
$$\begin{array}{r} 10 \\ + 2 \\ \hline \end{array}$$
$$\begin{array}{r} 8 \\ + 5 \\ \hline \end{array}$$
$$\begin{array}{r} 12 \\ - 5 \\ \hline \end{array}$$
$$\begin{array}{r} 11 \\ - 8 \\ \hline \end{array}$$
$$\begin{array}{r} 7 \\ + 6 \\ \hline \end{array}$$

4.
$$\begin{array}{r} 6 \\ + 7 \\ \hline \end{array}$$
$$\begin{array}{r} 13 \\ - 5 \\ \hline \end{array}$$
$$\begin{array}{r} 11 \\ - 6 \\ \hline \end{array}$$
$$\begin{array}{r} 8 \\ + 4 \\ \hline \end{array}$$
$$\begin{array}{r} 11 \\ - 9 \\ \hline \end{array}$$
$$\begin{array}{r} 13 \\ - 4 \\ \hline \end{array}$$

Know the addition facts (sums to 13) and the corresponding subtraction facts and commit them to memory

How Many Ways?

Circle ways to make **8**.

(4 + 4)

12 − 4

5 + 7

9 − 3

11 − 3

3 + 7

13 − 5

Circle ways to make **9**.

13 − 4

12 − 5

6 + 3

9 − 0

11 − 2

13 − 5

7 + 5

Circle ways to make **10**.

4 + 9

12 − 2

3 + 7

13 − 3

11 − 1

6 + 4

10 − 5

Circle ways to make **11**.

4 + 7

12 − 6

5 + 6

12 − 4

11 − 0

9 + 2

13 − 8

Circle ways to make **12**.

8 + 4

12 − 4

5 + 7

9 − 3

12 − 0

13 − 5

6 + 6

Circle ways to make **13**.

11 + 2

12 − 9

6 + 7

10 + 3

11 − 5

4 + 9

13 − 0

Know the addition facts (sums to 13) and the corresponding subtraction facts and commit them to memory

Number & Operations

EMC 3014 • Basic Math Skills, Grade 1 • ©2003 by Evan-Moor Corp.

Let's Eat!

Write the number sentence.

---

1. Jay ate 7 pancakes.
Amy ate 5 pancakes.
How many pancakes did
they eat in all?

____ ◯ ____ = ____

2. Mom made 13 waffles.
We ate 9 of them. How
many waffles were left?

____ ◯ ____ = ____

---

3. There were 12 eggs in the
carton. Mom cooked 7 of
them. How many eggs
were left?

____ ◯ ____ = ____

4. Pete and Kim put berries
on their cereal. Pete ate
6 berries. Kim ate 6 berries.
How many berries did they
eat in all?

____ ◯ ____ = ____

---

5. Write a word problem about this picture. Then write a number
sentence about it.

_____

_____

_____

____ ◯ ____ = ____

Know the addition facts (sums to 13) and the corresponding subtraction facts and commit them to memory

Math Test

Fill in the circle next to the correct answer.

1. $7 + 6 =$ _____
- Ⓐ 1
- Ⓑ 10
- Ⓒ 13
- Ⓓ 11

2. $8 + 3 =$ _____
- Ⓐ 12
- Ⓑ 11
- Ⓒ 8
- Ⓓ 3

3. $11 - 8 =$ _____
- Ⓐ 6
- Ⓑ 5
- Ⓒ 13
- Ⓓ 3

4. Which problem equals 13?
- Ⓐ $8 + 3$
- Ⓑ $8 + 4$
- Ⓒ $10 + 3$
- Ⓓ $5 + 7$

5. Which problem has the same answer as $12 - 9$?
- Ⓐ $0 + 6$
- Ⓑ $11 - 8$
- Ⓒ $6 + 6$
- Ⓓ $11 - 9$

6. Find the number sentence that is NOT correct.
- Ⓐ $13 - 5 = 4$
- Ⓑ $9 - 4 = 5$
- Ⓒ $12 - 3 = 9$
- Ⓓ $10 + 3 = 13$

7. Ross picked 9 carrots. He picked 4 squash. How many vegetables did Ross pick?
- Ⓐ 12
- Ⓑ 5
- Ⓒ 14
- Ⓓ 13

8. Find the number sentence for this picture.
- Ⓐ $7 - 6 = 1$
- Ⓑ $6 + 7 = 13$
- Ⓒ $13 - 3 = 10$
- Ⓓ $7 + 6 = 12$

Know the addition facts (sums to 13) and the corresponding subtraction facts and commit them to memory

Fly Away Home

Name _____

Show Mother Bird how to get to her nest. Color boxes with the answer **9** blue.

	$\begin{array}{r} 7 \\ +2 \\ \hline 9 \end{array}$	$\begin{array}{r} 8 \\ +4 \\ \hline \end{array}$	$\begin{array}{r} 9 \\ +5 \\ \hline \end{array}$	$\begin{array}{r} 10 \\ +5 \\ \hline \end{array}$	$\begin{array}{r} 14 \\ -9 \\ \hline \end{array}$
$\begin{array}{r} 11 \\ -6 \\ \hline \end{array}$	$\begin{array}{r} 12 \\ -3 \\ \hline \end{array}$	$\begin{array}{r} 13 \\ -3 \\ \hline \end{array}$	$\begin{array}{r} 6 \\ +9 \\ \hline \end{array}$	$\begin{array}{r} 14 \\ -7 \\ \hline \end{array}$	$\begin{array}{r} 7 \\ +5 \\ \hline \end{array}$
$\begin{array}{r} 12 \\ -0 \\ \hline \end{array}$	$\begin{array}{r} 15 \\ -6 \\ \hline \end{array}$	$\begin{array}{r} 5 \\ +4 \\ \hline \end{array}$	$\begin{array}{r} 8 \\ +6 \\ \hline \end{array}$	$\begin{array}{r} 5 \\ +9 \\ \hline \end{array}$	$\begin{array}{r} 15 \\ -8 \\ \hline \end{array}$
$\begin{array}{r} 11 \\ -7 \\ \hline \end{array}$	$\begin{array}{r} 8 \\ +5 \\ \hline \end{array}$	$\begin{array}{r} 14 \\ -5 \\ \hline \end{array}$	$\begin{array}{r} 8 \\ +3 \\ \hline \end{array}$	$\begin{array}{r} 15 \\ -5 \\ \hline \end{array}$	$\begin{array}{r} 7 \\ +8 \\ \hline \end{array}$
$\begin{array}{r} 7 \\ +4 \\ \hline \end{array}$	$\begin{array}{r} 12 \\ -7 \\ \hline \end{array}$	$\begin{array}{r} 11 \\ -2 \\ \hline \end{array}$	$\begin{array}{r} 13 \\ -4 \\ \hline \end{array}$	$\begin{array}{r} 6 \\ +3 \\ \hline \end{array}$	$\begin{array}{r} 13 \\ -7 \\ \hline \end{array}$
$\begin{array}{r} 14 \\ -8 \\ \hline \end{array}$	$\begin{array}{r} 15 \\ -7 \\ \hline \end{array}$	$\begin{array}{r} 7 \\ +6 \\ \hline \end{array}$	$\begin{array}{r} 8 \\ +4 \\ \hline \end{array}$	$\begin{array}{r} 15 \\ -6 \\ \hline \end{array}$	

Know the addition facts (sums to 15) and the corresponding subtraction facts and commit them to memory

Number & Operations

Under the Big Top

Name _____

Write all the answers.
Then connect the dots in order.
Start at answer **4**.

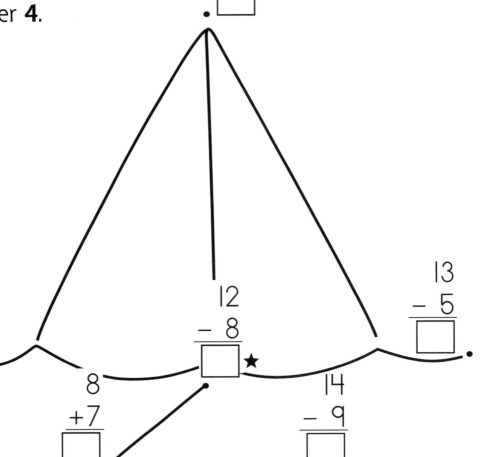

$$13$$
$$-\ 3$$

$$6$$
$$+5$$

$$8$$
$$+4$$

$$12$$
$$-\ 8$$

$$13$$
$$-\ 5$$

$$15$$
$$-\ 6$$

$$8$$
$$+7$$

$$14$$
$$-\ 9$$

$$7$$
$$+6$$

$$9$$
$$+5$$

$$15$$
$$-\ 9$$

$$14$$
$$-\ 7$$

Know the addition facts (sums to 15) and the corresponding subtraction facts and commit them to memory

EMC 3014 • Basic Math Skills, Grade 1 • ©2003 by Evan-Moor Corp.

Feed the Elephant

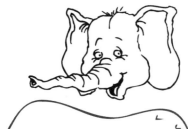

Write the answers.

1. $11 - 5 = 6$ $8 + 4 =$ $9 + 6 =$

2. $10 + 5 =$ $14 - 9 =$ $11 - 6 =$

3. $12 - 3 =$ $14 - 7 =$ $6 + 3 =$

4. $6 + 9 =$ $7 + 5 =$ $6 + 6 =$

5. $15 - 6 =$ $13 - 6 =$ $8 + 6 =$

6. $5 + 9 =$ $15 - 8 =$ $11 - 7 =$

The elephant ate the peanuts larger than **8**.
Circle those peanuts.

How many peanuts did the elephant eat? _____ peanuts

Know the addition facts (sums to 15) and the corresponding subtraction facts and commit them to memory

Number & Operations

It All Adds Up

Find pairs of numbers that add up to the sum on the crayon.
Circle each pair, using that color.

12 red

6	6	5	8	4
5	2	9	7	5
7	8	3	4	6

13 blue

8	7	6	4	9
5	3	9	7	5
6	7	4	2	8

14 green

5	9	3	8	6
4	6	4	7	7
4	8	9	5	0

15 purple

2	9	6	7	3
9	8	4	8	5
4	7	6	9	8

Know the addition facts (sums to 15) and the corresponding subtraction facts and commit them to memory

EMC 3014 • Basic Math Skills, Grade 1 • ©2003 by Evan-Moor Corp.

Don't Bug Me!

Name _____

Write the number sentence.

---

1. 15  were crawling. 8 stopped to take a nap. How many  were still crawling?

___ ◯ ___ = ___

2. 7  were flying. 6 more came. How many  were flying?

___ ◯ ___ = ___

---

3. 16  were eating grass. 9 hopped away. How many  were still eating grass?

___ ◯ ___ = ___

4. 7  were in the garden. 7 more came. How many  were in the garden?

___ ◯ ___ = ___

---

5. Write a word problem about this picture. Then write a number sentence about it.

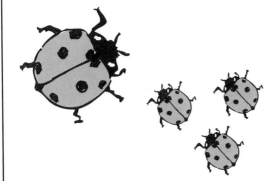

_____

_____

_____

___ ◯ ___ = ___

Know the addition facts (sums to 15) and the corresponding subtraction facts and commit them to memory

©2003 by Evan-Moor Corp. • Basic Math Skills, Grade 1 • EMC 3014

Number & Operations   **129**

Math Test

Fill in the circle next to the correct answer.

1. $7 + 8 =$ _____

  Ⓐ 13

  Ⓑ 15

  Ⓒ 14

  Ⓓ 12

2. $5 + 9 =$ _____

  Ⓐ 15

  Ⓑ 12

  Ⓒ 14

  Ⓓ 13

3. $14 - 7 =$ _____

  Ⓐ 7

  Ⓑ 8

  Ⓒ 9

  Ⓓ 6

4. $12 - 4 =$ _____

  Ⓐ 10

  Ⓑ 4

  Ⓒ 9

  Ⓓ 8

5. Which problem has the same answer as $12 - 4$?

  Ⓐ $12 + 4$

  Ⓑ $9 + 3$

  Ⓒ $3 + 8$

  Ⓓ $13 - 5$

6. Which number sentence is NOT correct?

  Ⓐ $6 + 7 = 13$

  Ⓑ $5 + 9 = 13$

  Ⓒ $7 + 6 = 13$

  Ⓓ $5 + 8 = 13$

7. Todd went fishing. He caught 9 small fish and 6 large fish. How many fish did he catch?

  Ⓐ 11

  Ⓑ 13

  Ⓒ 15

  Ⓓ 17

8. Find the number sentence for this picture.

  Ⓐ $12 - 6 = 6$

  Ⓑ $12 - 5 = 7$

  Ⓒ $12 - 4 = 8$

  Ⓓ $12 - 7 = 5$

Know the addition facts (sums to 15) and the corresponding subtraction facts and commit them to memory

What Kind of Horse Am I?

Name _____

Find the answers.
Connect the dots.
Start at **0**.

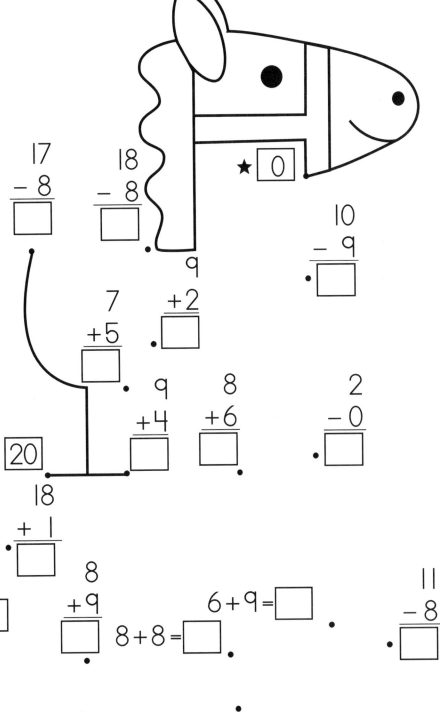

$15 - 7 =$ ☐

$\begin{array}{r} 17 \\ -\ 8 \\ \hline \square \end{array}$

$\begin{array}{r} 18 \\ -\ 8 \\ \hline \square \end{array}$

★ ☐ 0

$\begin{array}{r} 10 \\ -\ 9 \\ \hline \square \end{array}$

9

$\begin{array}{r} 7 \\ +5 \\ \hline \square \end{array}$

$\begin{array}{r} +2 \\ \hline \square \end{array}$

$\begin{array}{r} 9 \\ +4 \\ \hline \square \end{array}$

$\begin{array}{r} 8 \\ +6 \\ \hline \square \end{array}$

$\begin{array}{r} 2 \\ -0 \\ \hline \square \end{array}$

$16 - 9 =$ ☐

20

18

$\begin{array}{r} +\ 1 \\ \hline \square \end{array}$

$\begin{array}{r} 14 \\ -\ 8 \\ \hline \square \end{array}$

18

$\begin{array}{r} 8 \\ +9 \\ \hline \square \end{array}$

$6 + 9 =$ ☐

$8 + 8 =$ ☐

$\begin{array}{r} 11 \\ -\ 8 \\ \hline \square \end{array}$

$14 - 9 =$ ☐

$13 - 9 =$ ☐

I am a _____ horse.

Know the addition facts (sums to 20) and the corresponding subtraction facts and commit them to memory

©2003 by Evan-Moor Corp. • Basic Math Skills, Grade 1 • EMC 3014

What Is It?

What is black and white and red all over?

6–a	9–i	12–r	15–u
7–b	10–k	13–s	16–w
8–h	11–n	14–t	17–x

Use the code to solve the riddle.
Write the matching letter below each answer.

15 – 9	6 +7	20 – 10	8 +7	5 +6	16 – 6
6					
a					

8 +8	14 – 5	9 +5	15 – 7	16 –10

8 +5	6 +9	8 +3	17 –10	7 +8	8 +4	11 +0

Know the addition facts (sums to 20) and the corresponding subtraction facts and commit them to memory

In and Out

Name _____

Add 6	
5	11
6	
7	
8	
9	
10	

Subtract 6	
16	
15	
14	
13	
12	
11	

Add 9	
3	
4	
5	
6	
7	
8	

Subtract 9	
17	
16	
15	
14	
13	
12	

Add 8	
0	
2	
4	
6	
8	
10	

Subtract 8	
8	
10	
12	
14	
16	
18	

Add 10	
5	
6	
7	
8	
9	
10	

Subtract 10	
15	
16	
17	
18	
19	
20	

Know the addition facts (sums to 20) and the corresponding subtraction facts and commit them to memory

Number & Operations

Checking Subtraction

Name _____

Add to check the subtraction problems.

1.

$$\begin{array}{r} 18 \\ -\ 9 \\ \hline 9 \end{array} \quad \begin{array}{r} \boxed{9} \\ +\ 9 \\ \hline 18 \end{array}$$

$$\begin{array}{r} 16 \\ -\ 7 \\ \hline \end{array} \quad \begin{array}{r} \boxed{} \\ +\ 7 \\ \hline \end{array}$$

$$\begin{array}{r} 14 \\ -\ 9 \\ \hline \end{array} \quad \begin{array}{r} \boxed{} \\ +\ 9 \\ \hline \end{array}$$

$$\begin{array}{r} 12 \\ -\ 7 \\ \hline \end{array} \quad \begin{array}{r} \boxed{} \\ +\ 7 \\ \hline \end{array}$$

2.

$$\begin{array}{r} 14 \\ -\ 6 \\ \hline \end{array} \quad \begin{array}{r} \boxed{} \\ +\ 6 \\ \hline \end{array}$$

$$\begin{array}{r} 13 \\ -\ 8 \\ \hline \end{array} \quad \begin{array}{r} \boxed{} \\ +\ 8 \\ \hline \end{array}$$

$$\begin{array}{r} 17 \\ -\ 8 \\ \hline \end{array} \quad \begin{array}{r} \boxed{} \\ +\ 8 \\ \hline \end{array}$$

$$\begin{array}{r} 15 \\ -\ 7 \\ \hline \end{array} \quad \begin{array}{r} \boxed{} \\ +\ 7 \\ \hline \end{array}$$

3.

$$\begin{array}{r} 12 \\ -\ 4 \\ \hline \end{array} \quad \begin{array}{r} \boxed{} \\ +\ 4 \\ \hline \end{array}$$

$$\begin{array}{r} 16 \\ -\ 6 \\ \hline \end{array} \quad \begin{array}{r} \boxed{} \\ +\ 6 \\ \hline \end{array}$$

$$\begin{array}{r} 17 \\ -\ 9 \\ \hline \end{array} \quad \begin{array}{r} \boxed{} \\ +\ 9 \\ \hline \end{array}$$

$$\begin{array}{r} 13 \\ -\ 7 \\ \hline \end{array} \quad \begin{array}{r} \boxed{} \\ +\ 7 \\ \hline \end{array}$$

4.

$$\begin{array}{r} 16 \\ -\ 8 \\ \hline \end{array} \quad \begin{array}{r} \boxed{} \\ +\ 8 \\ \hline \end{array}$$

$$\begin{array}{r} 13 \\ -\ 6 \\ \hline \end{array} \quad \begin{array}{r} \boxed{} \\ +\ 6 \\ \hline \end{array}$$

$$\begin{array}{r} 15 \\ -\ 8 \\ \hline \end{array} \quad \begin{array}{r} \boxed{} \\ +\ 8 \\ \hline \end{array}$$

$$\begin{array}{r} 20 \\ -10 \\ \hline \end{array} \quad \begin{array}{r} \boxed{} \\ +10 \\ \hline \end{array}$$

Know the addition facts (sums to 20) and the corresponding subtraction facts and commit them to memory

EMC 3014 • Basic Math Skills, Grade 1 • ©2003 by Evan-Moor Corp.

At the Frog Pond

Name _____

---

1. 18 little frogs were sitting on a log. 9 frogs hopped away. How many frogs were left?

_____ frogs

Which did you do?

add   subtract

---

2. A bullfrog can jump 6 feet. How far will it go in 3 jumps?

_____ feet

Which did you do?

add   subtract

---

3. There were 17 flies. A frog ate 9 of them. How many flies were left?

_____ flies

Which did you do?

add   subtract

---

4. 6 frogs were in a pond. 7 more frogs came. How many frogs were in the pond?

_____ frogs

Which did you do?

add   subtract

---

5. Write a word problem about this picture. Then write a number sentence about it.

_____

_____

_____

_____ ◯ _____ = _____

Know the addition facts (sums to 20) and the corresponding subtraction facts and commit them to memory

Name _____

Math Test

Fill in the circle next to the correct answer.

1. 16 − 8 = _____
- Ⓐ 9
- Ⓑ 4
- Ⓒ 8
- Ⓓ 11

2. 10 + 9 = _____
- Ⓐ 1
- Ⓑ 19
- Ⓒ 16
- Ⓓ 9

3. Which problem has the same sum as 9 + 7?
- Ⓐ 8 + 9
- Ⓑ 12 − 8
- Ⓒ 6 + 5
- Ⓓ 7 + 9

4. Which problem has the same difference as 18 − 9?
- Ⓐ 14 − 7
- Ⓑ 16 − 7
- Ⓒ 18 − 7
- Ⓓ 15 − 7

5. Find the problem with the largest sum.
- Ⓐ 8 + 7
- Ⓑ 5 + 5
- Ⓒ 9 + 6
- Ⓓ 10 + 10

6. Carl invited 13 friends to his party. 4 could not come. How many friends were at his party?
- Ⓐ 8
- Ⓑ 17
- Ⓒ 9
- Ⓓ 7

7. Zack bought 4 apples, 6 oranges, and 5 bananas. How many apples and oranges does he have?
- Ⓐ 4 + 5 = 9
- Ⓑ 4 + 6 + 5 = 15
- Ⓒ 4 + 5 − 6 = 3
- Ⓓ 4 + 6 = 10

8. Lee is 6 years old. His sister is 15. How many years older is his sister?
- Ⓐ 6
- Ⓑ 7
- Ⓒ 8
- Ⓓ 9

Know the addition facts (sums to 20) and the corresponding subtraction facts and commit them to memory

Pat's Pet Puppy

Name _____

Write the answers.
Find the color for each answer.
Color the picture.

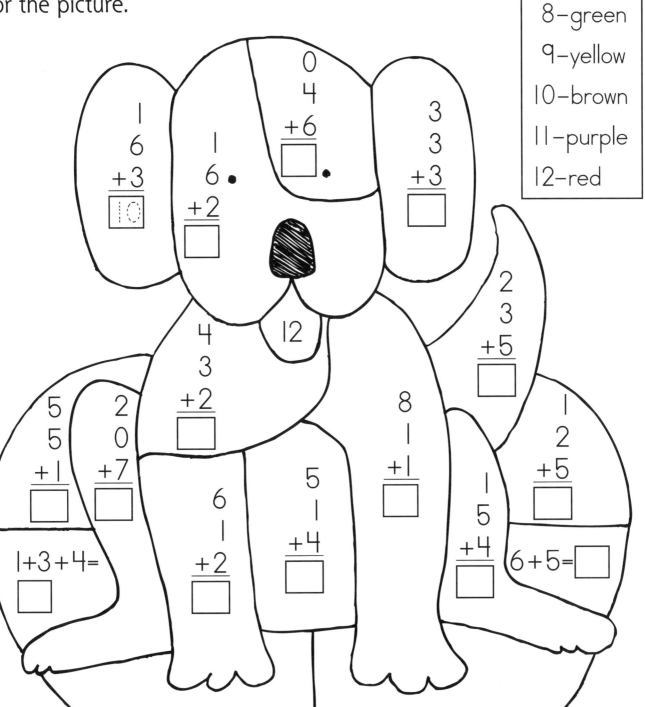

Find the sum of three one-digit numbers

Name _____

We carry our homes with us when we go for a walk.
Who are we?

4–a	7–l	10–s
5–e	8–n	11–t
6–i	9–r	12–u

Use the code to answer the riddle.
Write the matching letter below each answer.

1.

2 2 +6	3 4 +1	1 2 +1	3 0 +3	2 1 +4
10				
s				

2.

4 5 +2	3 6 +3	2 1 +6	7 3 +1	4 0 +3	2 1 +2

Find the sum of three one-digit numbers

Add Three Numbers

Name _____

Count the legs.
Then add the three numbers.

1.

2.

_____ + _____ + _____ = _____   _____ + _____ + _____ = _____

Add two numbers to make **10**. Then add the last number.

3.
$$\begin{matrix} 7 \\ 3 \end{matrix} \rangle \boxed{10}$$
$$+4 \quad +4$$
$$\quad \quad 14$$

4.
$$\begin{matrix} 1 \\ 9 \end{matrix} \rangle \boxed{}$$
$$+2 \quad +$$

5.
$$\begin{matrix} 8 \\ 2 \end{matrix} \rangle \boxed{}$$
$$+3 \quad +$$

Add doubles. Then add the last number.

6.
$$\begin{matrix} 3 \\ 3 \end{matrix} \rangle \boxed{6}$$
$$+9 \quad +9$$
$$\quad \quad 15$$

7.
$$\begin{matrix} 2 \\ 2 \end{matrix} \rangle \boxed{}$$
$$+8 \quad +$$

8.
$$\begin{matrix} 4 \\ 4 \end{matrix} \rangle \boxed{}$$
$$+2 \quad +$$

Find the sum of three one-digit numbers

1, 2, 3, What Will It Be?

Name _____

Find the answers.

1.

2 3 +4 ___ 9	2 2 +2	2 1 +3	3 2 +2	4 3 +3	8 2 +2

2.

6 3 +3	5 5 +2	1 5 +4	2 8 +1	3 3 +5	3 3 +3

3.

4 0 +9	6 2 +3	5 2 +3	4 4 +4	4 3 +7	8 0 +2

4.

4 1 +9	5 7 +3	2 4 +2	0 4 +3	5 4 +0	2 4 +1

5.

2 8 +4	2 3 +4	3 4 +3	5 2 +4	2 7 +2	4 6 +3

Find the sum of three one-digit numbers

Number & Operations

EMC 3014 • Basic Math Skills, Grade 1 • ©2003 by Evan-Moor Corp

Name _____

1. 3 campers went fishing. 5 campers went swimming. 4 campers went hiking. How many campers were there in all?

_____ campers

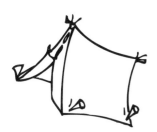

2. Raul is collecting leaves. He finds 4 red leaves. He finds 3 orange leaves. He finds 7 yellow leaves. How many leaves did he find in all?

_____ leaves

3. Kim, Candy, and Maria went fishing. Each girl caught 5 fish. How many fish did they catch in all?

_____ fish

4. Tony likes birds. Today he saw 7 jays, 3 hawks, and 4 quail. How many birds did he see?

_____ birds

5. Write a word problem about this picture. Then write a number sentence about it.

_____

_____

_____

_____ _____ _____ = _____

Find the sum of three one-digit numbers

Number & Operations

Math Test

Fill in the circle next to the correct answer.

1. $2 + 8 + 3 =$ _____

&Ⓐ 10

&Ⓑ 11

&Ⓒ 12

&Ⓓ 13

2. $4 + 4 + 5 =$ _____

&Ⓐ 9

&Ⓑ 12

&Ⓒ 14

&Ⓓ 13

3. $3 + 6 + 2 =$ _____

&Ⓐ 9

&Ⓑ 11

&Ⓒ 13

&Ⓓ 12

4. Which problem is NOT equal to fifteen?

&Ⓐ $5 + 6 + 4$

&Ⓑ $2 + 9 + 4$

&Ⓒ $1 + 7 + 5$

&Ⓓ $6 + 6 + 3$

5. Which problem has the same sum as $7 + 7$?

&Ⓐ $9 + 1 + 2$ Ⓒ $6 + 3 + 6$

&Ⓑ $8 + 3 + 2$ Ⓓ $7 + 3 + 4$

6. Bob saw 6 ants, 2 bees, and 3 butterflies. How many insects did he see?

&Ⓐ 15

&Ⓑ 11

&Ⓒ 12

&Ⓓ 14

7. Jill picked 3 roses, 3 daisies, and 3 tulips. How many flowers did she pick?

&Ⓐ 9

&Ⓑ 13

&Ⓒ 11

&Ⓓ 8

8. Find the number sentence for this picture.

&Ⓐ $6 + 4 + 3 = 13$

&Ⓑ $4 + 2 + 7 = 13$

&Ⓒ $5 + 4 + 4 = 13$

&Ⓓ $5 + 2 + 6 = 13$

Find the sum of three one-digit numbers

Barnyard Riddles

Name _____

Use the code to answer the riddles.
Write the matching letter below each sum or difference.

15–a	38–o	53–t
22–e	48–r	65–u
24–k	49–s	98–y

Use the code to answer the riddles.

What do you call a farmer's alarm clock?

36 +12	79 −41	18 +20	15 +34	67 − 14	58 −36	79 −31
48						
r						

What kind of key will you find in a barnyard?

89 −74	21 +32	23 +42	68 −20	66 −42	11 +11	61 +37

Solve addition and subtraction problems with two-digit numbers

Rescue the King

Name _____

Help the knight rescue the king from the dragon.
Color boxes with the answer **35** brown.

13 +22 35	10 +80	77 −65	59 −27	45 +54
46 −11	30 + 5	68 −33	36 +43	29 −16
33 +16	99 −46	59 −24	98 −63	25 +10
78 −44	55 −35	43 +22		

Solve addition and subtraction problems with two-digit numbers

Number & Operations   EMC 3014 • Basic Math Skills, Grade 1 • ©2003 by Evan-Moor Corp

Find the Answers

Name _____

Add or subtract the **ones** first.
Then add or subtract the **tens**.
Color the football with the largest answer in each row **brown**.

1. $\begin{array}{r} 24 \\ +50 \\ \hline 74 \end{array}$ $\begin{array}{r} 47 \\ +41 \\ \hline \end{array}$ $\begin{array}{r} 62 \\ -50 \\ \hline \end{array}$ $\begin{array}{r} 14 \\ +75 \\ \hline \end{array}$ $\begin{array}{r} 69 \\ -42 \\ \hline \end{array}$

2. $\begin{array}{r} 57 \\ -35 \\ \hline \end{array}$ $\begin{array}{r} 79 \\ -43 \\ \hline \end{array}$ $\begin{array}{r} 24 \\ +54 \\ \hline \end{array}$ $\begin{array}{r} 77 \\ -22 \\ \hline \end{array}$

3. $\begin{array}{r} 18 \\ +30 \\ \hline \end{array}$ $\begin{array}{r} 99 \\ -54 \\ \hline \end{array}$ $\begin{array}{r} 82 \\ +16 \\ \hline \end{array}$ $\begin{array}{r} 47 \\ -33 \\ \hline \end{array}$ $\begin{array}{r} 74 \\ -43 \\ \hline \end{array}$

4. $\begin{array}{r} 97 \\ -54 \\ \hline \end{array}$ $\begin{array}{r} 28 \\ +11 \\ \hline \end{array}$ $\begin{array}{r} 96 \\ -26 \\ \hline \end{array}$

Solve addition and subtraction problems with two-digit numbers

Which Are the Same?

Write the answers.
Circle the two problems in each
row that have the same answer.

Add or
subtract the
ones first.

1.

$$\begin{array}{r} 23 \\ +30 \\ \hline 53 \end{array}$$ $$\begin{array}{r} 42 \\ +43 \\ \hline \end{array}$$ $$\begin{array}{r} 65 \\ -50 \\ \hline \end{array}$$ $$\begin{array}{r} 16 \\ +72 \\ \hline \end{array}$$ $$\begin{array}{r} 47 \\ -32 \\ \hline \end{array}$$

2.

$$\begin{array}{r} 79 \\ -27 \\ \hline \end{array}$$ $$\begin{array}{r} 66 \\ -20 \\ \hline \end{array}$$ $$\begin{array}{r} 61 \\ +25 \\ \hline \end{array}$$ $$\begin{array}{r} 18 \\ +41 \\ \hline \end{array}$$ $$\begin{array}{r} 87 \\ -41 \\ \hline \end{array}$$

3.

$$\begin{array}{r} 15 \\ +34 \\ \hline \end{array}$$ $$\begin{array}{r} 34 \\ +13 \\ \hline \end{array}$$ $$\begin{array}{r} 96 \\ -52 \\ \hline \end{array}$$ $$\begin{array}{r} 26 \\ +23 \\ \hline \end{array}$$ $$\begin{array}{r} 99 \\ -11 \\ \hline \end{array}$$

Solve addition and subtraction problems with two-digit numbers

EMC 3014 • Basic Math Skills, Grade 1 • ©2003 by Evan-Moor Corp.

How Much Candy?

Write a number sentence to show the answer.

---

1. Carlos had 24 jelly beans. He gave 12 of the jelly beans to Kim. How many jelly beans did he have left?

____ ◯ ____ = ____

2. Maggie dropped her bag of gumdrops. 13 gumdrops fell on the table. 16 gumdrops fell on the floor. How many gumdrops did Maggie drop?

____ ◯ ____ = ____

---

3. Jamal loves gummi bears. His grandmother gave him a box of 36 gummi bears. He ate 25 of them. How many does he have left?

____ ◯ ____ = ____

4. Mrs. Gomez got candy for a piñata. She got 35 suckers. She got 21 candy kisses. How many pieces of candy did she get?

____ ◯ ____ = ____

---

5. Write a number story about this picture. Then write the number sentence.

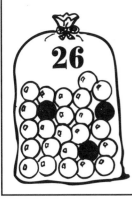

26   42

_____

_____

_____

____ ◯ ____ = ____

Solve addition and subtraction problems with two-digit numbers

Number & Operations

Math Test

Fill in the circle next to the correct answer.

1. 35 + 24 = _____
- Ⓐ 11
- Ⓑ 56
- Ⓒ 68
- Ⓓ 59

2. 58 + 20 = _____
- Ⓐ 68
- Ⓑ 78
- Ⓒ 88
- Ⓓ 38

3. 36 – 23 = _____
- Ⓐ 23
- Ⓑ 59
- Ⓒ 13
- Ⓓ 3

4. 85 – 35 = _____
- Ⓐ 40
- Ⓑ 50
- Ⓒ 99
- Ⓓ 35

5. Which problem has the same answer as 40 + 40?

30	60	90	4
+50	–10	–20	+40
Ⓐ	Ⓑ	Ⓒ	Ⓓ

6. Which problem has an answer that is more than 20 + 20?

15	49	26	34
+22	–34	+31	–13
Ⓐ	Ⓑ	Ⓒ	Ⓓ

7. Mark the problem that is NOT correct.

60	53	42	63
+18	+24	+47	+13
78	77	99	76
Ⓐ	Ⓑ	Ⓒ	Ⓓ

8. A big anteater ate 99 ants. A small anteater ate 36 ants. How many more ants did the big anteater eat than the small one?
- Ⓐ 36
- Ⓑ 63
- Ⓒ 53
- Ⓓ 60

Solve addition and subtraction problems with two-digit numbers

EMC 3014 • Basic Math Skills, Grade 1 • ©2003 by Evan-Moor Corp.

Algebra

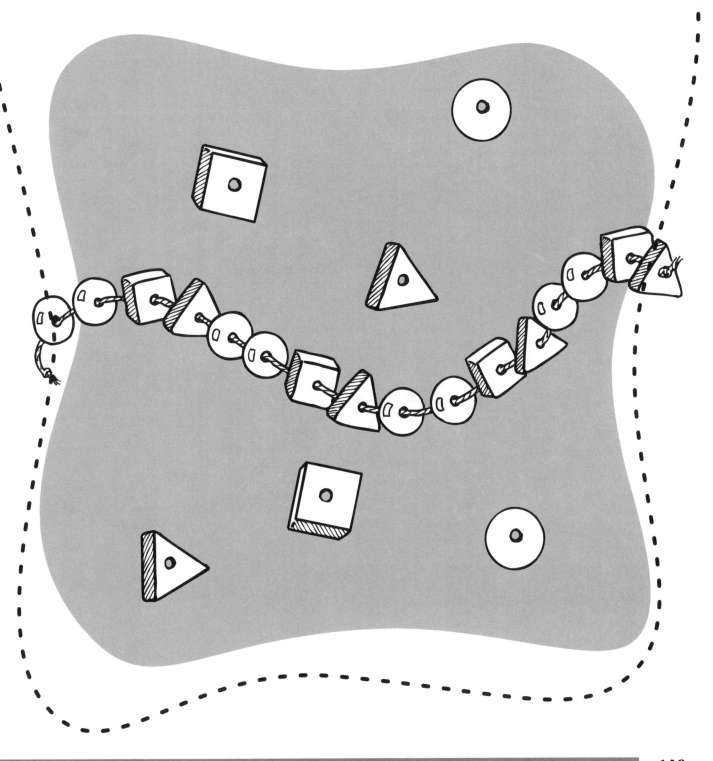

String of Beads

Color the beads.

red   **blue**   **yellow**

Copy the pattern.

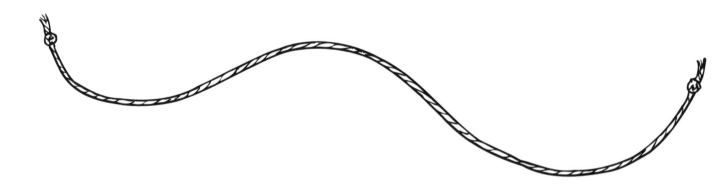

What is the name of the pattern? Circle it.

ABC   AABC   AABB   ABBC

Copy, extend, describe, and create patterns

150   Algebra

Scoops!

Color the ice cream.
Continue the pattern.

Make your own pattern. Use two or three colors.

1. orange / brown / red

2. brown / brown / pink

3. green / orange / orange

4.

Copy, extend, describe, and create patterns

Rows of Patterns

Circle the repeating unit.
Then use the letters **A**, **B**, and **C** to write the pattern.

1.

○ △ ○ △ ○ △ ○ △

A B A B A B A B

2.

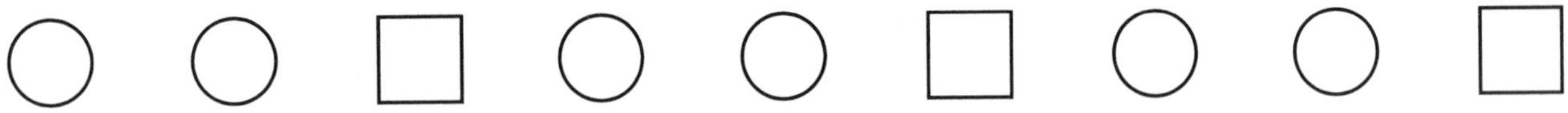

○ ○ □ ○ ○ □ ○ ○ □

____ ____ ____ ____ ____ ____ ____ ____ ____

3.

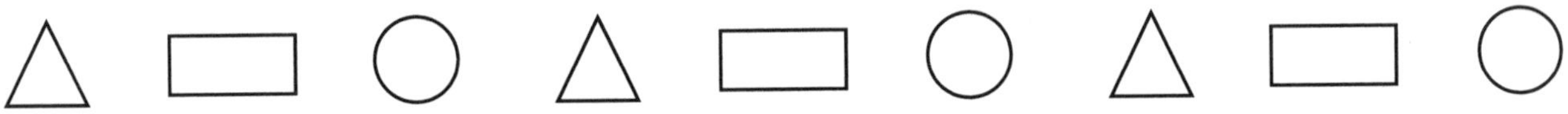

△ ▭ ○ △ ▭ ○ △ ▭ ○

____ ____ ____ ____ ____ ____ ____ ____ ____

4.

____ ____ ____ ____ ____ ____ ____ ____

5.

____ ____ ____ ____ ____ ____ ____ ____ ____

Draw an ABCABC pattern here.

____ ____ ____ ____ ____ ____ ____ ____ ____

Copy, extend, describe, and create patterns

Extend the Pattern

1. ○ ○ □ ○ ○ □ ___ ___ ___ ___ ___ ___

2. ○ ○ ○ ○ ○ ○ ___ ___ ___ ___ ___ ___ ___

3. ■ ▲ □ ■ ▲ □ ___ ___ ___ ___

4. ★ ★ ♥ ☾ ★ ★ ♥ ☾ ★ ___ ___ ___ ___

5. 2 4 8 2 4 8 2 4 8 ___ ___ ___ ___ ___ ___ ___

6. ___ ___ ___ ___ ___ ___

7. ___ ___ ___ ___ ___ ___

Copy, extend, describe, and create patterns

Pattern Challenge

Name _____

1. Color the balloons to make a pattern.
   The pattern must have 3 yellow and 6 red balloons.

2. Color the bears to show a pattern.
   Use three colors.

3. Color the flowers to show a pattern.
   Use three colors. Flowers 1 and 5 must be the same color.

4. Draw a pattern using a ◯ and ☐.
   The pattern must be different from the others.

Copy, extend, describe, and create patterns

EMC 3014 • Basic Math Skills, Grade 1 • ©2003 by Evan-Moor Corp.

Math Test

Fill in the circle next to the correct answer.

1. What comes next?

○ ○ □ ○ ○ ___ ___

Ⓐ □ □

Ⓑ ○ □

Ⓒ □ ○

Ⓓ □ △

2. What comes next?

2, 4, 6, 8, ___

Ⓐ 14

Ⓑ 10

Ⓒ 12

Ⓓ 16

3. What comes next?

XXYZXX ___ ___

Ⓐ YZ

Ⓑ XYZ

Ⓒ ZXX

Ⓓ XXY

4. What pattern is this?

□ ○ □ ○ □ ○

Ⓐ ABCABC

Ⓑ ABABAB

Ⓒ AABAAB

Ⓓ ABACAB

5. Find the ABBABB pattern.

Ⓐ ○ △ △ ○ △ △

Ⓑ ○ △ □ ○ △ □

Ⓒ ○ △ ○ ○ △ ○

Ⓓ ○ ○ △ ○ ○ △

6. What pattern is this?

Ⓐ ABABAB

Ⓑ AABBAABB

Ⓒ AABAAB

Ⓓ ABBABB

7. What is the repeating unit?

XXOXXO

Ⓐ XO

Ⓑ XOO

Ⓒ XXO

Ⓓ OOX

8. What is the repeating unit?

○ △ □ ○ △ □

Ⓐ ○ ○ △

Ⓑ □ ○ □

Ⓒ ○ □ △

Ⓓ ○ △ □

Copy, extend, describe, and create patterns

Baby Bear's Porridge

Name _____

Help Baby Bear get to his food. Write the missing signs.
Color the addition problems yellow.

	2 □ 2 4	3 □ 3 6	10 □ 3 7	18 □ 9 9
10 □ 5 5	14 □ 7 7	4 □ 4 8	12 □ 3 9	11 □ 8 3
6 □ 6 0	15 □ 1 14	5 □ 5 10	14 □ 5 9	12 □ 5 7
13 □ 8 5	16 □ 9 7	6 □ 6 12	7 □ 7 14	10 □ 9 1
11 □ 2 9	13 □ 4 9	12 □ 6 6	8 □ 8 16	10 □ 5 5
13 □ 7 6	17 □ 9 8	12 □ 12 0	9 □ 9 18	

Use the symbols +, −, and = correctly

Algebra

EMC 3014 • Basic Math Skills, Grade 1 • ©2003 by Evan-Moor Corp.

Crawly Caterpillars

Name _____

Write the missing numbers and signs.

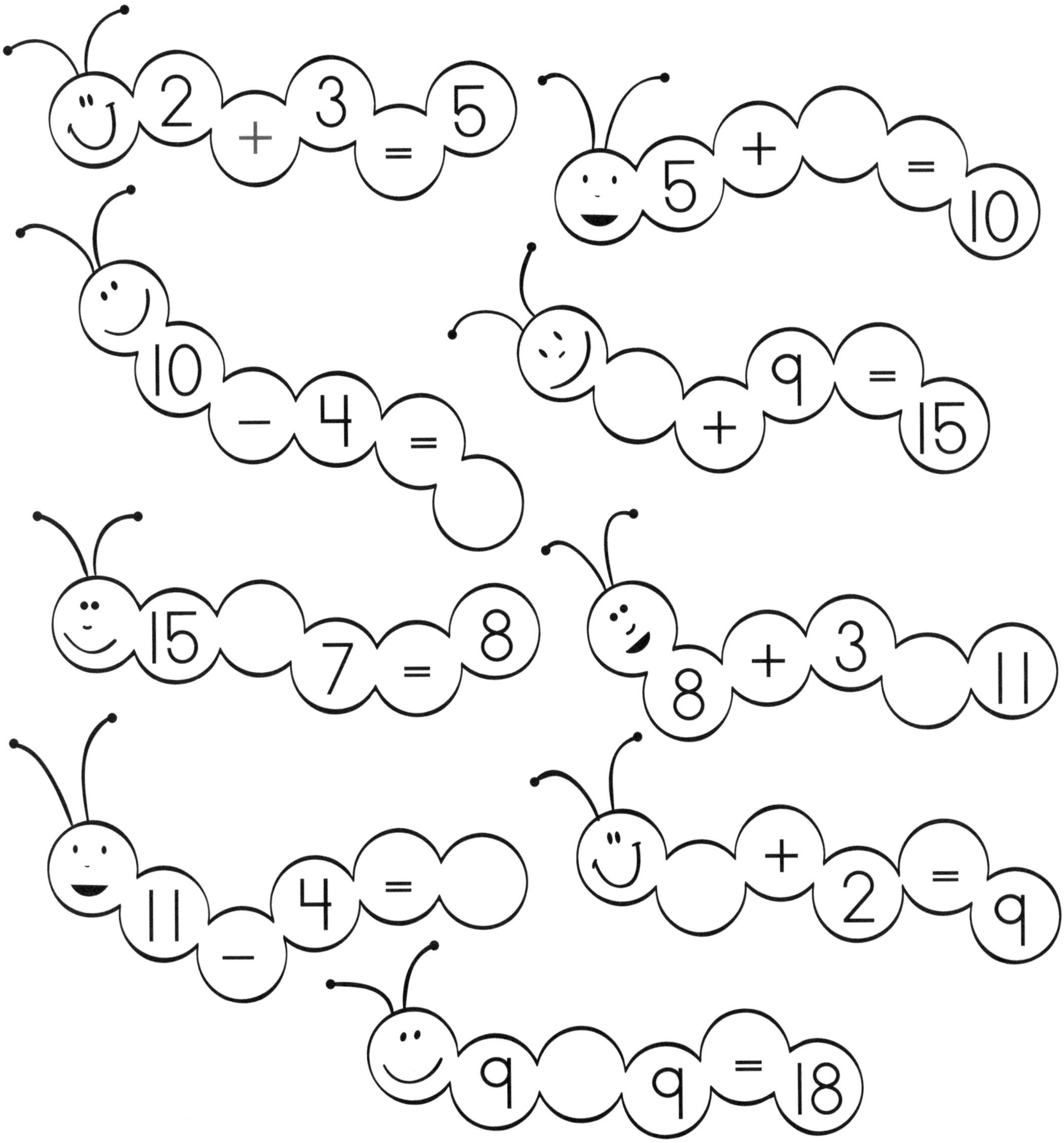

$2 + 3 = 5$

$5 + = 10$

$10 - 4 = $

$ + 9 = 15$

$15 7 = 8$

$8 + 3 11$

$11 - 4 = $

$ + 2 = 9$

$9 9 = 18$

Use the symbols +, −, and = correctly

Plus or Minus?

Name _____

What sign is missing?
Write **+** or **−**.

1.
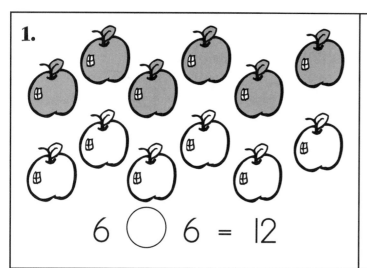

6 ◯ 6 = 12

2.
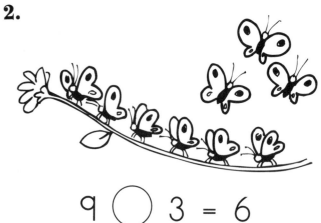

9 ◯ 3 = 6

3.

10 ◯ 8 = 18

4.
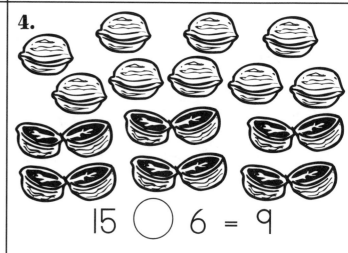

15 ◯ 6 = 9

5.
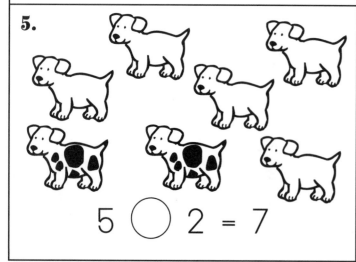

5 ◯ 2 = 7

6.
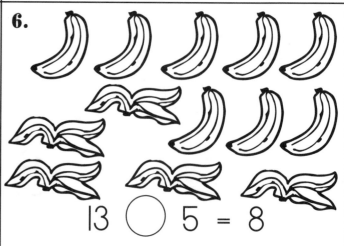

13 ◯ 5 = 8

Use the symbols +, −, and = correctly

Algebra

EMC 3014 • Basic Math Skills, Grade 1 • ©2003 by Evan-Moor Corp.

What's My Sign?

Name _____

Read the problem. Write the correct sign in the box.

+ −

6 ⊡ 6 12	4 ☐ 8 12	11 ☐ 5 6	12 ☐ 9 3
2 ☐ 9 11	10 ☐ 6 16	6 ☐ 7 13	10 ☐ 8 2
8 ☐ 3 11	12 ☐ 7 5	6 ☐ 9 15	13 ☐ 6 7
4 ☐ 9 13	11 ☐ 3 8	9 ☐ 4 13	15 ☐ 15 0
15 ☐ 9 6	11 ☐ 2 9	8 ☐ 6 14	3 ☐ 7 10
14 ☐ 8 6	12 ☐ 4 8	6 ☐ 8 14	15 ☐ 7 8

Use the symbols +, −, and = correctly

©2003 by Evan-Moor Corp. • Basic Math Skills, Grade 1 • EMC 3014

Algebra

Scrambled Sentences

Name _____

Oh no! The teacher dropped the cards! Help her unscramble them. Write the number sentences correctly.

1. | 11 | 6 | 5 | − | = |

| 11 | − | 6 | = | 5 |

2. | 7 | 4 | 3 | = | + |

| | | | | |

3. | 4 | = | + | 9 | 13 |

| | | | | |

4. | − | 8 | 15 | = | 7 |

| | | | | |

5. | 17 | 8 | 9 | = | + |

| | | | | |

6. | = | 6 | 13 | 7 | − |

| | | | | |

Use the symbols +, −, and = correctly

EMC 3014 • Basic Math Skills, Grade 1 • ©2003 by Evan-Moor Corp.

Math Test

Fill in the circle next to the correct answer.

1. $17 - 9 =$ _____

- Ⓐ 26
- Ⓑ 16
- Ⓒ 8
- Ⓓ 2

2. $12 + 6 =$ _____

- Ⓐ 6
- Ⓑ 18
- Ⓒ 4
- Ⓓ 16

3. Which sign is missing?

$$9 \bigcirc 8 = 17$$

- Ⓐ =
- Ⓑ −
- Ⓒ +

4. Which sign is missing?

$$15 \bigcirc 7 = 8$$

- Ⓐ =
- Ⓑ −
- Ⓒ +

5. Which sign is missing?

$$11 - 3 \bigcirc 8$$

- Ⓐ =
- Ⓑ −
- Ⓒ +

6. Which number sentence uses these signs and numbers correctly?

$$= + 7\ 5\ 2$$

- Ⓐ $7 + 2 = 5$
- Ⓑ $7 - 5 = 2$
- Ⓒ $5 + 7 = 2$
- Ⓓ $2 + 5 = 7$

7. Which sign means "add"?

- Ⓐ =
- Ⓑ −
- Ⓒ +

8. Which sign means "subtract"?

- Ⓐ =
- Ⓑ −
- Ⓒ +

Use the symbols +, −, and = correctly

Fishing for Facts

Name _____

1. Cut out the fish.

2. Put them facedown in the bowl.

3. Take **2** fish.

4. Write a **+** problem.

5. Write a **−** problem.

6. Pick **2** new numbers.

Add

____ + ____ = ____

____ + ____ = ____

____ + ____ = ____

____ + ____ = ____

Subtract

____ − ____ = ____

____ − ____ = ____

____ − ____ = ____

____ − ____ = ____

Write, solve, and create problem situations involving addition and subtraction

Algebra   EMC 3014 • Basic Math Skills, Grade 1 • ©2003 by Evan-Moor Corp.

Ball Toss

It is your job to keep score.
Each player tossed a ball two times.
The number line shows how many
points the player won. Add the
points together to find the total
points won.

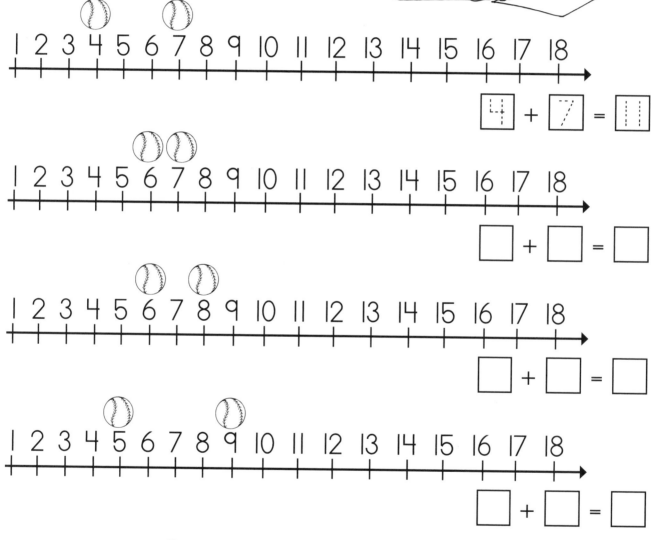

1 2 3 4 5 6 7 8 9 10 11 12 13 14 15 16 17 18

$\boxed{4} + \boxed{7} = \boxed{11}$

1 2 3 4 5 6 7 8 9 10 11 12 13 14 15 16 17 18

$\boxed{} + \boxed{} = \boxed{}$

1 2 3 4 5 6 7 8 9 10 11 12 13 14 15 16 17 18

$\boxed{} + \boxed{} = \boxed{}$

1 2 3 4 5 6 7 8 9 10 11 12 13 14 15 16 17 18

$\boxed{} + \boxed{} = \boxed{}$

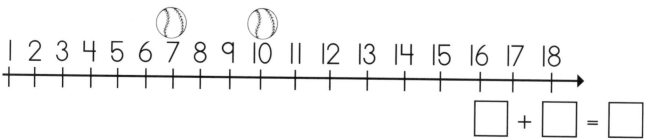

1 2 3 4 5 6 7 8 9 10 11 12 13 14 15 16 17 18

$\boxed{} + \boxed{} = \boxed{}$

Write, solve, and create problem situations involving addition and subtraction

What Is Missing?

Look at how much you have. Look at how much you need.
Write and draw the missing amount.

1.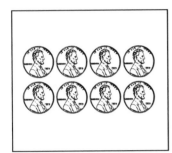

$$8¢ + \rule{1.5cm}{0.4pt}¢ = 10¢$$

2.

$$9¢ + \rule{1.5cm}{0.4pt}¢ = 16¢$$

3.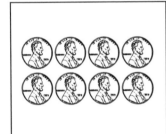

$$8¢ + \rule{1.5cm}{0.4pt}¢ = 14¢$$

4.

$$9¢ + \rule{1.5cm}{0.4pt}¢ = 12¢$$

Fill in the missing amount.

5. $8¢ + \rule{1.5cm}{0.4pt}¢ = 13¢$

6. $9¢ + \rule{1.5cm}{0.4pt}¢ = 13¢$

7. $5¢ + \rule{1.5cm}{0.4pt}¢ = 15¢$

8. $4¢ + \rule{1.5cm}{0.4pt}¢ = 11¢$

9. $10¢ + \rule{1.5cm}{0.4pt}¢ = 20¢$

10. $7¢ + \rule{1.5cm}{0.4pt}¢ = 14¢$

11. $8¢ + \rule{1.5cm}{0.4pt}¢ = 16¢$

12. $5¢ + \rule{1.5cm}{0.4pt}¢ = 10¢$

Write, solve, and create problem situations involving addition and subtraction

EMC 3014 • Basic Math Skills, Grade 1 • ©2003 by Evan-Moor Corp.

At the Beach

Find out what happened to me at the beach.
Draw a picture to solve each problem.
Write a number sentence about it.

I saw 2 sailboats.
I saw 1 ship. How
many boats did
I see?

2 (+) 1 = 3

1. I found 4 big shells. I found 9 little shells. How many shells did I find?

____ ◯ ____ = ____

2. I saw 10 birds walking on the beach. 6 birds flew away. How many birds were left?

____ ◯ ____ = ____

3. I caught 12 little fish. I let 8 of them go. How many fish did I have left?

____ ◯ ____ = ____

4. I played with 5 boys and 6 girls at the beach. How many children did I play with at the beach?

____ ◯ ____ = ____

Write, solve, and create problem situations involving addition and subtraction

Balloons and Bubbles

Name _____

1. Write an addition (+) problem about balloons. Draw a picture about it. Then write the number sentence.

I have 6 balloons. I get 7 more. How many balloons do I have?		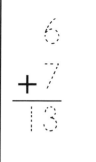

2. Write a subtraction (–) problem about balloons. Draw a picture about it. Then write the number sentence.

_____ _____ _____ _____		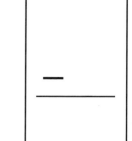

3. Write an addition problem about bubbles. Draw a picture about it. Then write the number sentence.

_____ _____ _____ _____		

Write, solve, and create problem situations involving addition and subtraction

Algebra   EMC 3014 • Basic Math Skills, Grade 1 • ©2003 by Evan-Moor Corp.

Name _____

Math Test

Fill in the circle next to the correct answer.

1. Bill found 6 big rocks. He found 9 little rocks. How many rocks did he find?

Ⓐ 3
Ⓑ 14
Ⓒ 15
Ⓓ 6

2. 6 boys and 8 girls went on a hike. How many children went on a hike?

Ⓐ 2
Ⓑ 4
Ⓒ 12
Ⓓ 14

3. 12 sheep were eating grass. 7 ran away. How many sheep were still eating grass?

Ⓐ 19
Ⓑ 5
Ⓒ 9
Ⓓ 14

4. Steve saw 12 birds on the way to school. He saw 14 birds on the way home. How many birds did he see in all?

2   36   26   28
Ⓐ   Ⓑ   Ⓒ   Ⓓ

5. Kim had 14 cherries. She ate 9 of them. How many cherries did she have left?

5   15   23   6
Ⓐ   Ⓑ   Ⓒ   Ⓓ

6. Sandy had 6 balloons. She gave 6 balloons to her friends. How many balloons did she have left?

6   12   2   0
Ⓐ   Ⓑ   Ⓒ   Ⓓ

7. What is the number sentence for this picture?

Ⓐ 5 + 3 = 8
Ⓑ 8 – 3 = 5
Ⓒ 8 – 4 = 4
Ⓓ 8 + 3 = 5

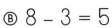
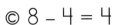
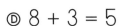

8. What is the number sentence for this picture?

Ⓐ 10 + 7 = 3
Ⓑ 10 – 3 = 7
Ⓒ 3 + 10 = 7
Ⓓ 7 – 3 = 10

Write, solve, and create problem situations involving addition and subtraction

Geometry

EMC 3014 • Basic Math Skills, Grade 1 • ©2003 by Evan-Moor Corp.

Dragonfly

Color the shapes.

◯ red

▢ blue

△ orange

▢ yellow

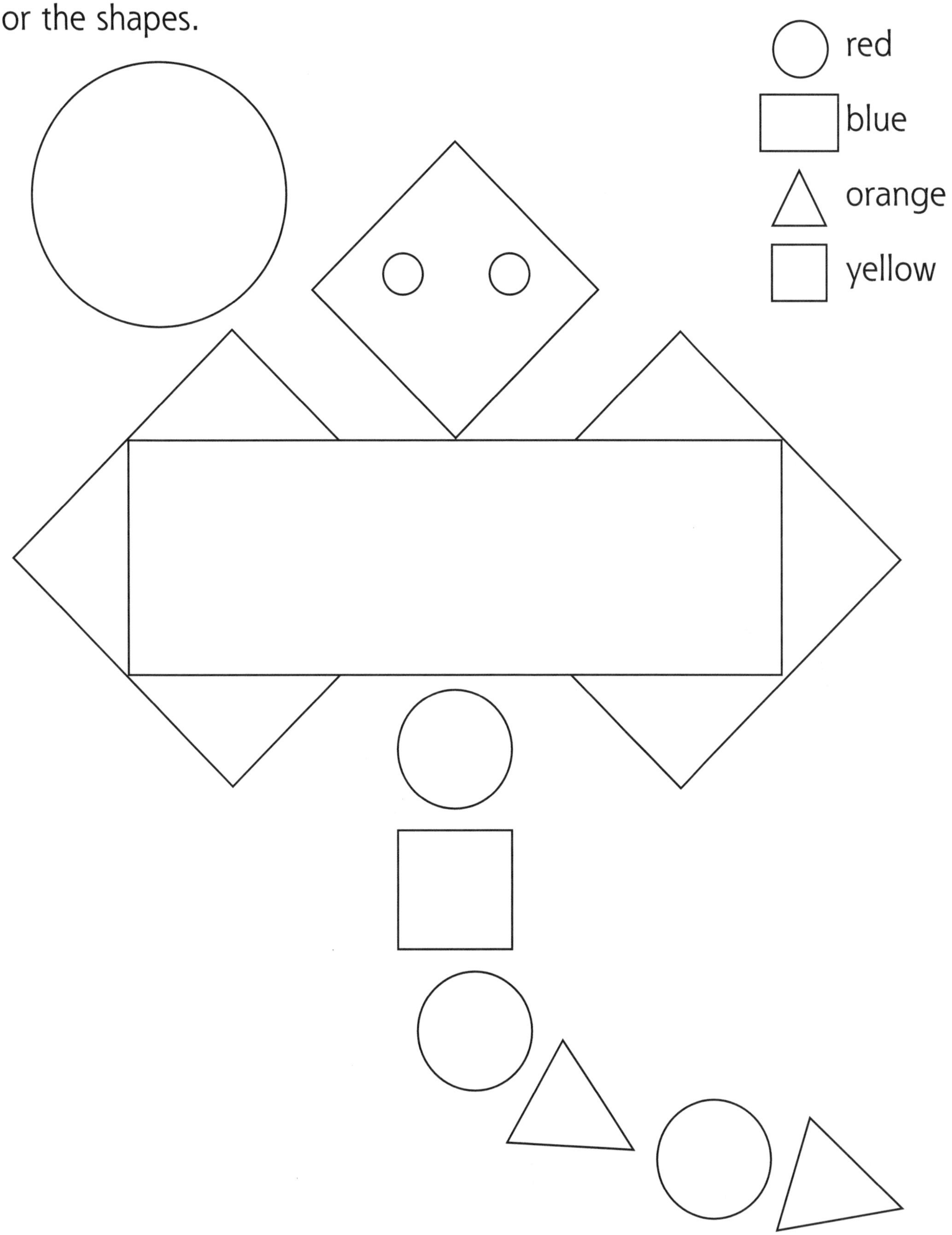

Identify, describe, and compare plane objects (triangles, rectangles, squares, and circles)

Look Both Ways

Name _____

Use this code to solve the riddle.

△ – d	▭ – h	■ – r
● – e	▲ – i	△ – s
□ – g	▪ – o	● – t

Why did the
chicken cross
the road?

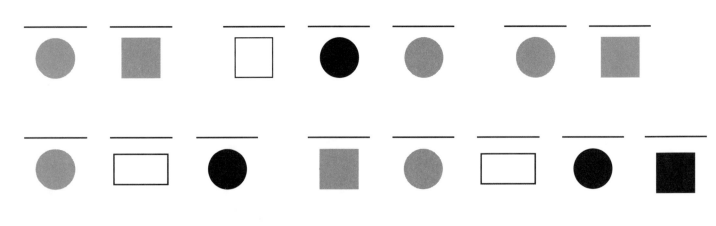

Identify, describe, and compare plane objects (triangles, rectangles, squares, and circles)

Which Shape Is It?

Name _____

square   **triangle**   **rectangle**   **circle**

Name the shapes. Tell how many sides and corners.
Draw the sides **red**. Make a black **X** on the corners.

1.

_____
name

_____ sides _____ corners

2.

_____
name

_____ sides _____ corners

3.

_____
name

_____ sides _____ corners

4.

_____
name

_____ sides _____ corners

5.

_____
name

_____ sides _____ corners

6.

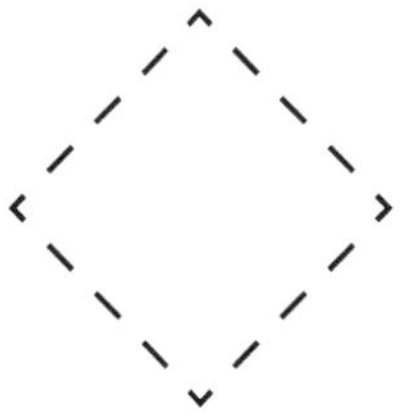

_____
name

_____ sides _____ corners

Identify, describe, and compare plane objects (triangles, rectangles, squares, and circles)

I Can Draw Shapes!

Read how many sides and corners.
Draw the shape.

1. 4 sides 4 corners	**2.** 3 sides 3 corners
3. 4 equal sides 4 corners	**4.** 0 sides 0 corners

5. How are a ☐ and a ☐ alike?

_____

6. How are a ☐ and a ☐ different?

_____

Identify, describe, and compare plane objects (triangles, rectangles, squares, and circles)

A Super Shape Surprise

Name _____

Use these shapes to draw a surprise picture.

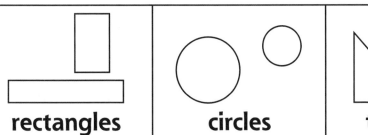  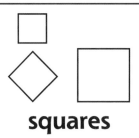

| rectangles | circles | triangles | squares |

How many of each shape did you use?

 ____    ____    ____    ____

Identify, describe, and compare plane objects (triangles, rectangles, squares, and circles)

Fill in the circle next to the correct answer.

1. Find the circle.

Ⓐ ☐
Ⓑ ▭
Ⓒ ◯
Ⓓ △

2. Find the triangle.

Ⓐ ▭
Ⓑ △
Ⓒ ☐
Ⓓ ◯

3. Find the rectangle.

Ⓐ ◯
Ⓑ ☐
Ⓒ △
Ⓓ ▭

4. Find the square.

Ⓐ ☐
Ⓑ ▭
Ⓒ ◯
Ⓓ △

5. What shape is this slice of pizza?

Ⓐ square
Ⓑ circle
Ⓒ triangle
Ⓓ rectangle

6. What shape is this piece of paper?

Ⓐ square
Ⓑ circle
Ⓒ triangle
Ⓓ rectangle

7. I have 4 sides that are all the same size. What am I?

Ⓐ ▭
Ⓑ ◯
Ⓒ ☐
Ⓓ △

8. I have no sides and no corners. What am I?

Ⓐ ◯
Ⓑ ☐
Ⓒ △
Ⓓ ▭

Identify, describe, and compare plane objects (triangles, rectangles, squares, and circles)

Color the Shapes

Name _____

 - black    - blue   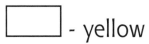 - yellow   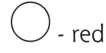 - red

 - orange   - purple   - pink   - green

Come One!
Come All!
See the
Balancing
Dog!

Classify familiar plane and solid objects by common attributes

Jump, Frogs, Jump!

Name _____

These frogs like to jump on different shapes.
Color the shapes.

1. This frog jumps only on shapes that can roll.

2. This frog jumps only on shapes that can NOT roll.

 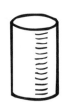 

3. This frog jumps only on shapes that can be stacked on each other.

 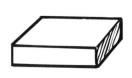 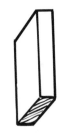  

4. This frog jumps only on shapes that can NOT be stacked on each other.

     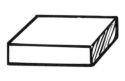

Classify familiar plane and solid objects by common attributes

EMC 3014 • Basic Math Skills, Grade 1 • ©2003 by Evan-Moor Corp.

Which Go Together?

Name _____

Match the shapes.

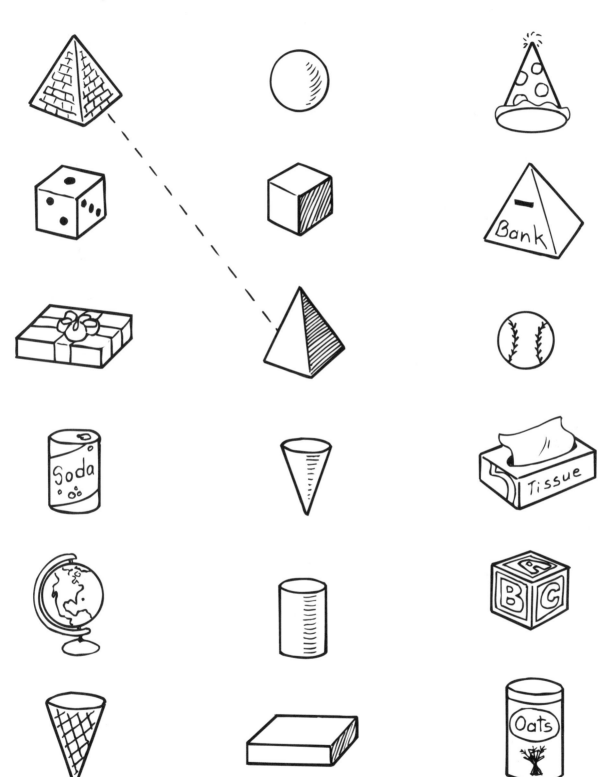

Classify familiar plane and solid objects by common attributes

Looking for Shapes

1. Color the **cones** red.
How do you know which shapes are cones?

_____

2. Color the **cubes** green.
How do you know which shapes are cubes?

_____

3. Color the **spheres** orange.
How do you know which shapes are spheres?

_____

4. Color the **cylinders** purple.
How do you know which shapes are cylinders?

_____

Outline this part of the solid shape.

circle   square   triangle   rectangle

   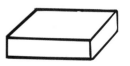

Classify familiar plane and solid objects by common attributes

Shape Search

Look around the classroom.
Find objects that are the shapes below.
Make an **X** by a shape you can find.
Draw it in the box.

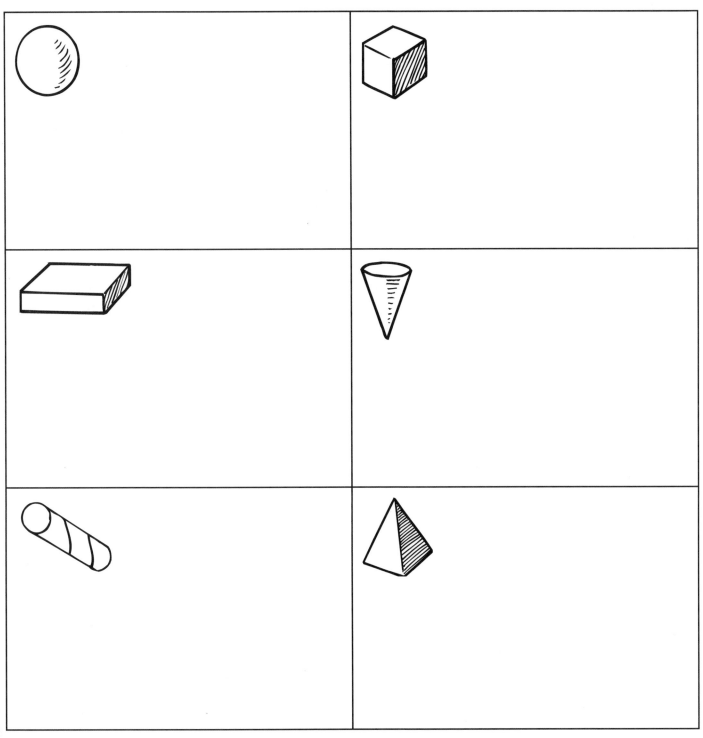

Classify familiar plane and solid objects by common attributes

Math Test

Fill in the circle next to the correct answer.

1. Find the sphere.

Ⓐ   Ⓑ   Ⓒ   Ⓓ

2. Find the cone.

Ⓐ   Ⓑ   Ⓒ   Ⓓ

3. Find the cube.

Ⓐ   Ⓑ   Ⓒ   Ⓓ

4. Find the pyramid.

Ⓐ   Ⓑ   Ⓒ   Ⓓ

5. Which object has flat ends and can roll?

Ⓐ   Ⓑ   Ⓒ   Ⓓ

6. Which object has the same shape?

   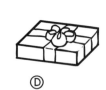

Ⓐ   Ⓑ   Ⓒ   Ⓓ

7. Which object has the same shape?

Ⓐ   Ⓑ   Ⓒ   Ⓓ

8. One side of a cube is a _____.
    Ⓐ rectangle
    Ⓑ triangle
    Ⓒ square
    Ⓓ circle

Classify familiar plane and solid objects by common attributes

An Apple Tree

Read and color.

1. Color the bird on **top** of the tree black.

2. Color the sun to the **left** of the tree yellow.

3. Color the apples **under** the bird red.

4. Color the dog **next to** the tree brown.

5. Color the apples on the **left** side of the tree green.

6. Color the grass **under** the tree green.

7. Draw a yellow cat on the **right** side of the tree.

Give and follow directions about location

Geometry

At the Petting Zoo

Name _____

Use the map. Draw a line along the path.

1. Start at the horse. Go **right**. What animal do you see? _____

2. Go **down** to the turtle. What animal did you go past? _____

3. Go **left** from the turtle. What animal do you see? _____

4. Go **up** to the next animal. What animal do you see? _____

5. Go to the **right**. What animal do you see? _____

6. Go **up**. What animal do you see? _____

Give and follow directions about location

EMC 3014 • Basic Math Skills, Grade 1 • ©2003 by Evan-Moor Corp.

Find the Lost Puppy

Name _____

Help Maurice find his lost puppy.

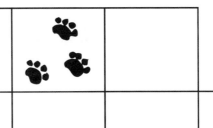

Start at the ★.
Go **right** 4 boxes.
What do you see? _____

Go **down** 2 boxes.
What do you see? _____

Go **right** 3 boxes.
What do you see? _____

Go **up** 4 boxes.
What do you see? _____

Give and follow directions about location

At School

Name _____

Read and follow the directions.

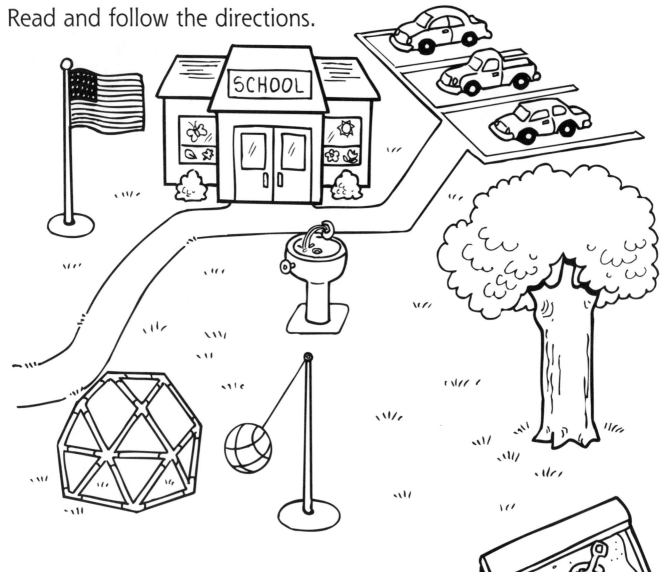

1. What is **above** the drinking fountain?
   Color it red.

2. What is to the **left** of the school building?
   Color it red, white, and blue.

3. What is **below** the parking lot?
   Color it green and brown.

4. What is right **below** the drinking fountain?
   Color it yellow and black.

5. Draw a child in the sandbox.

Give and follow directions about location

EMC 3014 • Basic Math Skills, Grade 1 • ©2003 by Evan-Moor Corp.

Secret Object

Tell how to find a secret object.

1. Pick a big object in your classroom. It should be on the floor.

2. Write directions from the door to the object. Use words from the Word Box.

3. Draw a picture to show the way.

Word Box			
around	over	between	left
right	beside	next to	under

Directions:

Start at the door. _____

_____

_____

_____

_____

_____

_____

Draw a picture on the back of this page to show the way.

Give and follow directions about location

Name _____

Math Test

Fill in the circle next to the correct answer.

1. Which arrow points right?

Ⓐ ←
Ⓑ →
Ⓒ ↑
Ⓓ ↓

2. Which arrow points down?

Ⓐ ←
Ⓑ →
Ⓒ ↑
Ⓓ ↓

3. Which arrow points left?

Ⓐ ←
Ⓑ →
Ⓒ ↑
Ⓓ ↓

4. Which arrow points up?

Ⓐ ←
Ⓑ →
Ⓒ ↑
Ⓓ ↓

5. Where is the cat?

Ⓐ over the tree
Ⓑ in the tree
Ⓒ next to the tree
Ⓓ behind the tree

6. Start at the star. Go right 5 boxes. What do you see?

Ⓐ ball
Ⓑ bone
Ⓒ heart
Ⓓ flower

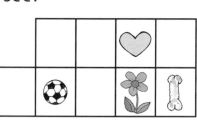

7. Start at the star. Go right 2 boxes. Go up 1 box. Go right 2 boxes. What do you see?

Ⓐ ball
Ⓑ bone
Ⓒ heart
Ⓓ flower

8. Start at the star. Where is the ball?

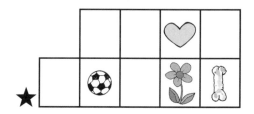

Ⓐ right 4 boxes
Ⓑ left 2 boxes
Ⓒ right 5 boxes
Ⓓ right 2 boxes

Give and follow directions about location

EMC 3014 • Basic Math Skills, Grade 1 • ©2003 by Evan-Moor Corp.

I Love a Parade

Name _____

Color and cut out the clowns.
Glue them in a row.
Use words from the Word Box to tell
where the clowns are in the row.

Word Box

left	right
between	next to

glue here	glue here	glue here	glue here	glue here

1. The red clown is _____.

2. The yellow clown is _____.

3. The green clown is _____.

red   blue   green   brown   yellow

Arrange and describe objects in space by proximity, position, and direction

Flower Garden

Color and cut out the flowers.
Glue them in the garden.
Use words from the Word Box
to tell where the flowers are in
the garden.

Word Box

left	right
between	next to
in front of	behind

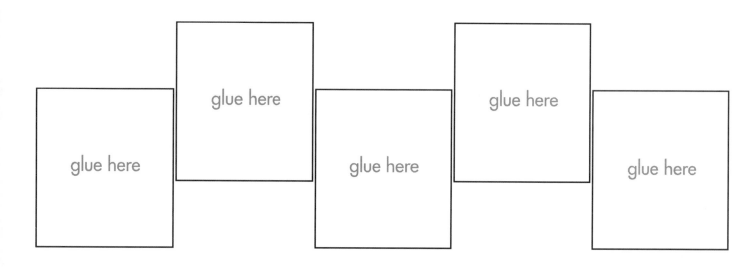

1. The blue flower is _____

2. The orange flower is _____.

3. The purple flower is _____.

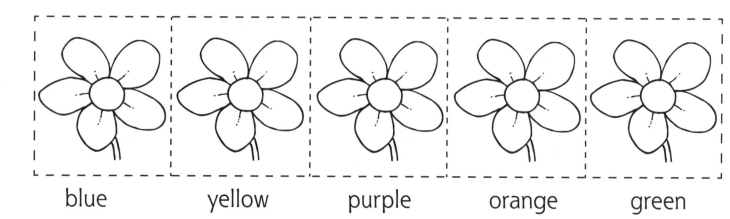

blue   yellow   purple   orange   green

Arrange and describe objects in space by proximity, position, and direction

Find the Shapes

Draw each shape in a different box.

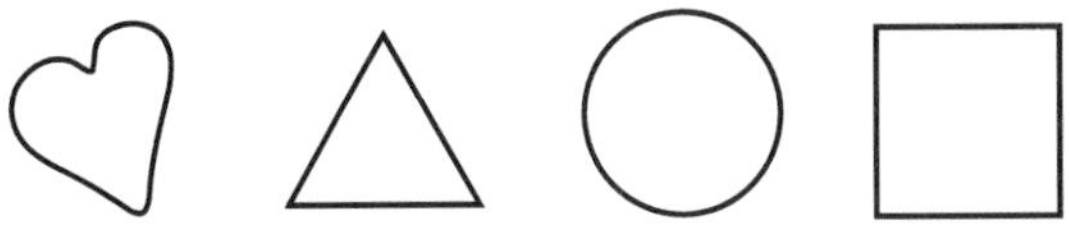

♡ △ ○ ▢

(grid with flower in center box, star at bottom left)

Write directions to each shape. Always start at the star.
The first one has been done for you.

🌼 Go right 2 boxes. Go up 1 box. _____.

♡ _____.

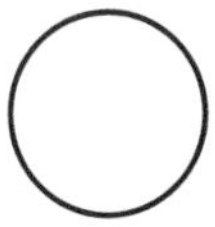

○ _____.

△ _____.

▢ _____.

Arrange and describe objects in space by proximity, position, and direction

Which Way?

Name _____

Draw a picture in three boxes on the grid.
Write directions to each picture. Always start at the star.
Ask a friend to read the directions to find the pictures.

★

_____

_____

_____

_____

_____

Arrange and describe objects in space by proximity, position, and direction

EMC 3014 • Basic Math Skills, Grade 1 • ©2003 by Evan-Moor Corp.

The Playground

Name _____

Draw a picture of your school's playground.
Use words from the box to help tell where the objects are.

Word Box

left

right

between

next to

on

in front of

behind

over

under

_____

_____

_____

_____

_____

Arrange and describe objects in space by proximity, position, and direction

Math Test

Fill in the circle next to the correct answer.

1. Where is the fish?

Ⓐ behind the dog

Ⓑ in front of the cat

Ⓒ under the dog

Ⓓ between the cat and dog

2. Where is the cat?

Ⓐ in front of the fish

Ⓑ over the dog

Ⓒ in front of the dog

Ⓓ under the fish

3. What is between the cat and the fish?

Ⓐ dog

Ⓑ fish

Ⓒ cat

Ⓓ rabbit

4. Where is the square?

Ⓐ over the triangle

Ⓑ between the circle and triangle

Ⓒ next to the square

Ⓓ under the circle

5. Where is the triangle?

Ⓐ over the circle

Ⓑ between the circle and square

Ⓒ under the circle

Ⓓ under the square

6. Where is the 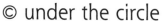?

Ⓐ behind the flower

Ⓑ in front of the heart

Ⓒ between the heart and flower

Ⓓ under the heart

7. Start at the star. Go right 3 boxes. What do you see?

Ⓐ   Ⓑ   Ⓒ   Ⓓ

8. How can you get to the heart? Start at the star.

Ⓐ Go right 2 boxes.

Ⓑ Go right 3 boxes. Go up 1 box.

Ⓒ Go right 2 boxes. Go up 1 box.

Ⓓ Go right 4 boxes.

Arrange and describe objects in space by proximity, position, and direction

EMC 3014 • Basic Math Skills, Grade 1 • ©2003 by Evan-Moor Corp.

Are Both Sides the Same?

Name _____

Circle **yes** if both sides are the same.
Circle **no** if the sides are not the same.

1. yes (no)

2. yes no

3. yes no

4. yes no

5. yes no

6. yes no

7. yes no

8. yes no

9. yes no

When an item is **symmetrical**, both sides are the same shape and size.

Identify and draw lines of symmetry

Fill the Baskets

Draw a line from each picture to the correct basket.

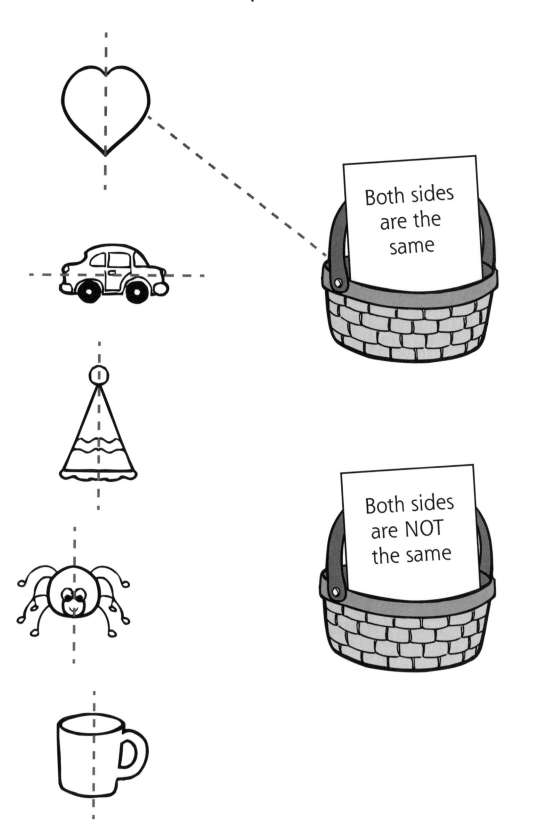

Identify and draw lines of symmetry

EMC 3014 • Basic Math Skills, Grade 1 • ©2003 by Evan-Moor Corp.

Both Sides Match

Name _____

Draw a line to show two sides exactly the same.

Mark the crackers three different ways to show halves that match.

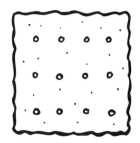 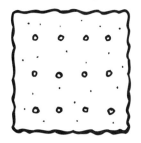 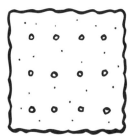

Identify and draw lines of symmetry

©2003 by Evan-Moor Corp. • Basic Math Skills, Grade 1 • EMC 3014

Geometry

Draw the Other Side

Make it symmetrical.

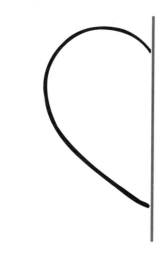

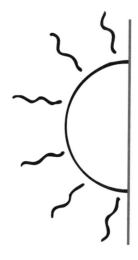

Identify and draw lines of symmetry

Geometry

EMC 3014 • Basic Math Skills, Grade 1 • ©2003 by Evan-Moor Corp.

Check Your Clothes

Name _____

Mrs. Lee works in a factory that makes clothing.
She checks to see that both sides match.
Look at your clothes.

Find something where both
sides match. Draw it here.

Find something where the sides
do NOT match. Draw it here.

Identify and draw lines of symmetry

Name _____

Fill in the circle next to the correct answer.

1. Which shape is the same on both sides?

Ⓐ Ⓒ

Ⓑ Ⓓ

2. Which shape is the same on both sides?

Ⓐ 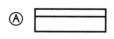 Ⓒ

Ⓑ  Ⓓ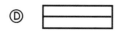

3. Which shape is NOT the same on both sides?

Ⓐ Ⓒ

Ⓑ Ⓓ

4. Which shape is NOT the same on both sides?

Ⓐ Ⓒ

Ⓑ Ⓓ

5. Which shape is the other side of this heart?

Ⓐ Ⓑ Ⓒ Ⓓ

6. Which shape is the other side of this hat?

Ⓐ   Ⓑ   Ⓒ   Ⓓ

7. This shape is NOT symmetrical. Why?

Ⓐ the sides are the same size
Ⓑ the sides are the same shape
Ⓒ the sides are different shapes
Ⓓ one side is darker

8. This shape is symmetrical. Why?

Ⓐ one side is darker
Ⓑ the sides are different sizes
Ⓒ the sides are different shapes
Ⓓ the sides are the same shape and size

Identify and draw lines of symmetry

Measurement

Animal Parade

Name _____

Number the animals from the shortest to the tallest.

_____   _____   _____   _____

Draw one animal that is shorter than the mouse.

Draw one animal that is taller than the zebra.

Compare length using direct comparison or nonstandard units

Monkey Measure

Name _____

How do these animals measure up to monkeys?
Cut out the monkeys. Use them to measure.

1. About how tall is the giraffe?

_____ monkeys tall

2. About how long is the snake?

_____ monkeys long

3. About how wide is the elephant?

_____ monkeys wide

Compare length using direct comparison or nonstandard units

Measurement

Dog Bone Measuring

Name _____

Help Dizzy Dog measure his things.
How long is each thing?

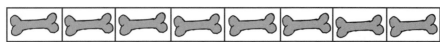 _____

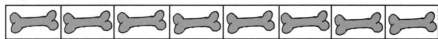 _____

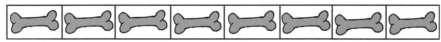 _____

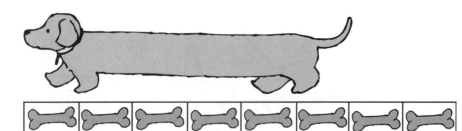

_____

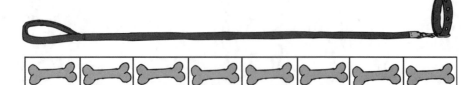

_____

Compare length by using direct comparison or nonstandard units

EMC 3014 • Basic Math Skills, Grade 1 • ©2003 by Evan-Moor Corp

How Long Is It?

You need a  to do this page.

Use it to measure each picture.

1.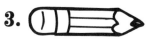

_____ paper clips long

2.

_____ paper clips long

3.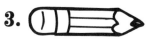

_____ paper clip long

4.

_____ paper clips long

5.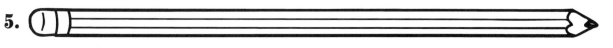

_____ paper clips long

6.

_____ paper clip long

7. About how many paper clips long is your pencil?

_____ paper clips long

Compare length using direct comparison or nonstandard units

Use a Shoe

Take off one shoe.
Use it to measure things
in your classroom.

My desk is
8 shoes wide.

---

your desk

How wide? _____ shoes

your chair

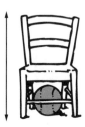

How tall? _____ shoes

a bookcase

How wide? _____ shoes

a backpack

How wide? _____ shoes

a door

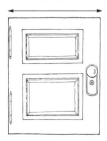

How wide? _____ shoes

a friend

How tall? _____ shoes

Compare length using direct comparison or nonstandard units

EMC 3014 • Basic Math Skills, Grade 1 • ©2003 by Evan-Moor Corp

Math Test

Fill in the circle next to the correct answer.

1. Which pencil is the longest?

- Ⓐ
- Ⓑ
- Ⓒ
- Ⓓ

2. Which pencil is the shortest?

- Ⓐ
- Ⓑ
- Ⓒ
- Ⓓ

3. Which boy is the tallest?

Ⓐ   Ⓑ   Ⓒ   Ⓓ

4. Which ribbon is the longest?

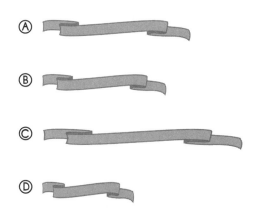

5. How wide is the apple?

- Ⓐ 6 dots wide
- Ⓑ 3 dots wide
- Ⓒ 2 dots wide
- Ⓓ 4 dots wide

6. How tall is the tree?

- Ⓐ 5 boxes tall
- Ⓑ 6 boxes tall
- Ⓒ 7 boxes tall
- Ⓓ 8 boxes tall

7. How long is the snake?

- Ⓐ 7 paper clips long
- Ⓑ 8 paper clips long
- Ⓒ 9 paper clips long
- Ⓓ 10 paper clips long

8. How wide is the bookshelf?

- Ⓐ 5 socks wide
- Ⓑ 6 socks wide
- Ⓒ 7 socks wide
- Ⓓ 8 socks wide

Compare length using direct comparison or nonstandard units

Big Foot

Take off your shoe and stand on this paper.
Trace around your foot.

Cut out the ruler and measure your foot.

1. My foot is _____ inches wide. **2.** My foot is _____ inches long.

Measure length using customary (inch) or metric (centimeter) units

My Hand

Name _____

Trace around your hand on this paper.
Cut out the ruler and measure your hand.

1. My hand is _____ centimeters wide.

2. My hand is _____ centimeters long.

3. My thumb is _____ centimeters long.

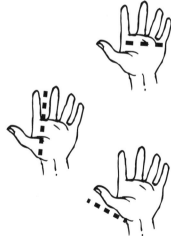

1	2	3	4	5	6	7	8	9	10	11	12	13	14	15

Measure length using customary (inch) or metric (centimeter) units

Tool Time

Measure.

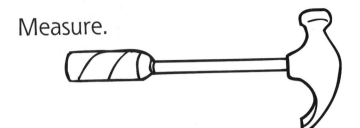

_____ inches

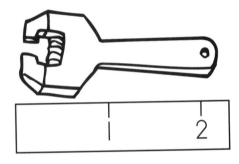

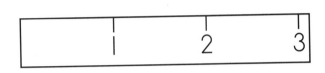

_____ inches

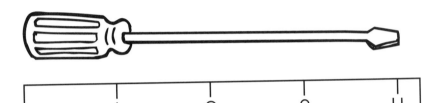

_____ inches

_____ inches

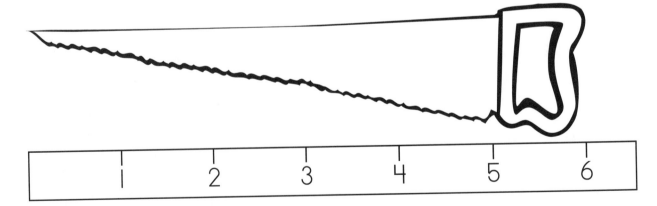

_____ inches

Measure length using customary (inch) or metric (centimeter) units

   EMC 3014 • Basic Math Skills, Grade 1 • ©2003 by Evan-Moor Corp

Let's Eat!

Measure.

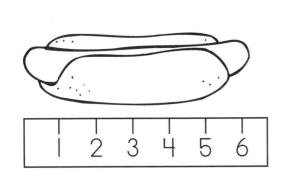

| 1 | 2 | 3 | 4 | 5 | 6 |

_____ centimeters

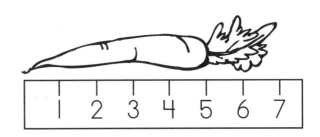

| 1 | 2 | 3 | 4 | 5 | 6 | 7 |

_____ centimeters

| 1 | 2 |

_____ centimeters

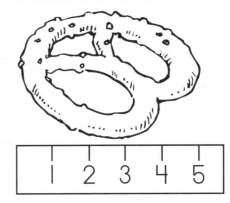

| 1 | 2 | 3 | 4 | 5 |

_____ centimeters

_____ centimeters

| 1 | 2 | 3 | 4 |

_____ centimeters

Measure length using customary (inch) or metric (centimeter) units

Measure and Compare

Name _____

Measure.
Write the number sentence.

---

1. Look at the baby mice. How much longer is the white mouse?

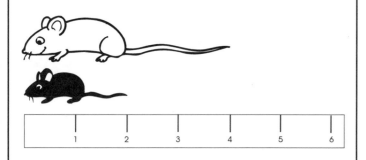

| | | | | | |
|1|2|3|4|5|6|

_____ ◯ _____ = _____

---

2. Look at the two bugs. How much longer is the worm?

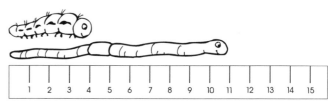

|1|2|3|4|5|6|7|8|9|10|11|12|13|14|15|

_____ ◯ _____ = _____

---

3. Look at the two lizards. How much longer is the gray lizard?

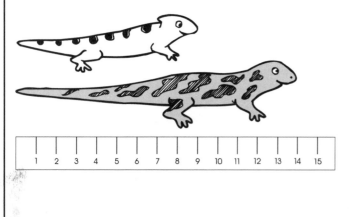

|1|2|3|4|5|6|7|8|9|10|11|12|13|14|15|

_____ ◯ _____ = _____

---

4. Look at how far these two bugs jumped. How much farther did the 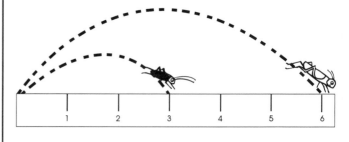 jump?

|1|2|3|4|5|6|

_____ ◯ _____ = _____

Measure length using customary (inch) or metric (centimeter) units

EMC 3014 • Basic Math Skills, Grade 1 • ©2003 by Evan-Moor Corp

Name _____

Fill in the circle next to the correct answer.

1. How long is it?

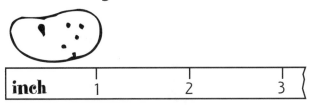

- Ⓐ 1 inch
- Ⓑ 2 inches
- © 3 inches
- Ⓓ 4 inches

2. How long is it?

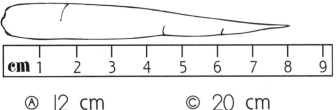

- Ⓐ 12 cm
- Ⓑ 16 cm
- © 20 cm
- Ⓓ 8 cm

3. How long is it?

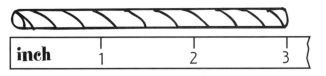

- Ⓐ 2 inches
- Ⓑ 3 inches
- © 4 inches
- Ⓓ 5 inches

4. How long is it?

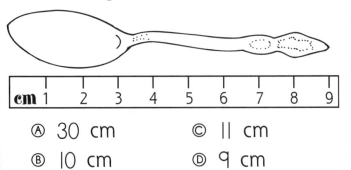

- Ⓐ 30 cm
- Ⓑ 10 cm
- © 11 cm
- Ⓓ 9 cm

5. How wide is it?

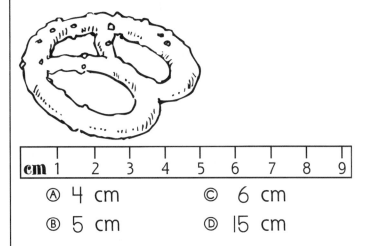

- Ⓐ 4 cm
- Ⓑ 5 cm
- © 6 cm
- Ⓓ 15 cm

6. How long is it?

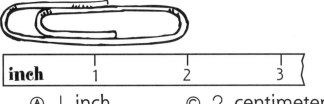

- Ⓐ 1 inch
- Ⓑ 1 centimeter
- © 2 centimeters
- Ⓓ 2 inches

7. How many inches are on the ruler?

- Ⓐ 1 inch
- Ⓑ 2 inches
- © 3 inches
- Ⓓ 4 inches

8. How many centimeters are on the ruler?

- Ⓐ 8 centimeters
- Ⓑ 9 centimeters
- © 10 centimeters
- Ⓓ 12 centimeters

Measure length using customary (inch) or metric (centimeter) units

Measurement

Seesaw

Name _____

Look at each seesaw.
Circle the heaviest animal.
Make an **X** on the lightest one.

1.

2.

3.

4.

Compare weight or liquid volume using direct comparison or nonstandard units

EMC 3014 • Basic Math Skills, Grade 1 • ©2003 by Evan-Moor Corp

Weighing In

Color the animal that weighs more.

1.

2.

3.

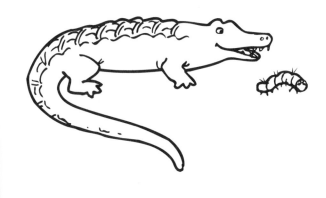

4.

5.

6.

Compare weight or liquid volume using direct comparison or nonstandard units

Fill Them Up

Name _____

Would you use a  or a 🥛 to fill each container?
Circle the answer.

1.	**2.**	**3.**
spoon cup	spoon cup	spoon cup
4.	**5.**	**6.**
spoon cup	spoon cup	spoon cup
7.	**8.**	**9.**
spoon cup	spoon cup	spoon cup

Compare weight or liquid volume using direct comparison or nonstandard units

Measurement   EMC 3014 • Basic Math Skills, Grade 1 • ©2003 by Evan-Moor Corp.

How Much Do They Weigh?

Name _____

Janet used blocks to weigh her fruit.
How much did each fruit weigh?

1.

_____ **blocks**

2.

_____ **blocks**

3.

_____ **blocks**

4.

_____ **blocks**

Compare weight or liquid volume using direct comparison or nonstandard units

Which Holds More?

Name _____

Circle the one that holds more.

1.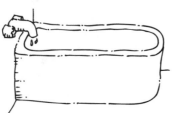

2.

3.

4.

5.

6.

Compare weight or liquid volume using direct comparison or nonstandard units

EMC 3014 • Basic Math Skills, Grade 1 • ©2003 by Evan-Moor Corp.

Name _____

Math Test

Fill in the circle next to the correct answer.

1. Which one weighs the most?

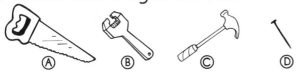

Ⓐ   Ⓑ   Ⓒ   Ⓓ

2. Which one weighs the least?

Ⓐ   Ⓑ   Ⓒ   Ⓓ

3. Which one holds the most water?

Ⓐ   Ⓑ   Ⓒ   Ⓓ

4. Which one holds the least water?

Ⓐ   Ⓑ   Ⓒ   Ⓓ

5. Which one holds the most juice?

Ⓐ   Ⓑ   Ⓒ   Ⓓ

6. Which one holds the least juice?

Ⓐ   Ⓑ   Ⓒ   Ⓓ

7. What does this seesaw show?

Ⓐ They weigh the same.
Ⓑ The bunny weighs more.
Ⓒ The bear weighs more.
Ⓓ The bear weighs less than the bunny.

8. What does this scale show?

Ⓐ The apple weighs 10 blocks.
Ⓑ The apple weighs 12 blocks.
Ⓒ The apple weighs 4 blocks.
Ⓓ The apple weighs 8 blocks.

Compare weight or liquid volume using direct comparison or nonstandard units

Measurement

Complete the Clock

Fill in the missing numbers on the clock.

Circle the clocks you have in your house.

Tell time to the nearest half hour and relate time to events

EMC 3014 • Basic Math Skills, Grade 1 • ©2003 by Evan-Moor Corp.

Tick Tock Goes the Clock

Name _____

Cut out the puzzle pieces.
Glue them on top of the matching clocks.

What does the puzzle show? _____

Tell time to the nearest half hour and relate time to events

I Can Tell Time

Name _____

Draw lines to match each clock to the correct time.

8:30

5:00

2:00

10:30

3:30

6:00

1:30

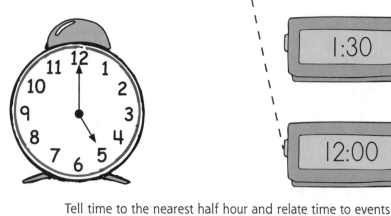

12:00

Tell time to the nearest half hour and relate time to events

Measurement   EMC 3014 • Basic Math Skills, Grade 1 • ©2003 by Evan-Moor Corp.

What Time Is It?

Name _____

Tell the time.

1.

____ : ____

2.

____ : ____

3.

____ : ____

4.

____ : ____

5.

____ : ____

6.

____ : ____

7.

____ : ____

8.

____ : ____

9.

____ : ____

Tell time to the nearest half hour and relate time to events

Measurement

Keeping Track of the Time

Name _____

Keep track of the time for one day.
Show the time you do each thing.

_____ 's Day
(your name)

The time I got up. 		
The time school started. 		
The time I ate lunch. 		
The time school ended. 		
The time I went to bed. 		

Tell time to the nearest half hour and relate time to events

222

Measurement

EMC 3014 • Basic Math Skills, Grade 1 • ©2003 by Evan-Moor Corp.

Math Test

Fill in the circle next to the correct answer.

1. What time is it?
- Ⓐ 12:00
- Ⓑ 4:30
- Ⓒ 3:00
- Ⓓ 4:00

2. What time is it?
- Ⓐ 9:30
- Ⓑ 9:00
- Ⓒ 8:30
- Ⓓ 10:00

3. What time is it?
- Ⓐ 12:30
- Ⓑ 5:00
- Ⓒ 7:00
- Ⓓ 6:00

4. What time is it?
- Ⓐ 12:30
- Ⓑ 1:30
- Ⓒ 2:30
- Ⓓ 3:30

5. What time is it?
- Ⓐ 6:00
- Ⓑ 12:30
- Ⓒ 11:00
- Ⓓ 11:30

6. Which clock shows 12:00?

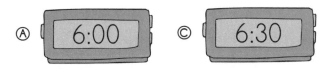

Ⓐ 6:00   Ⓒ 6:30

Ⓑ 12:30   Ⓓ 12:00

7. Which clock shows 6:30?

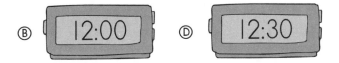

Ⓐ 6:00   Ⓒ 6:30

Ⓑ 12:00   Ⓓ 12:30

8. Ann went to the park at 10:00. She came home one hour later. At what time did she come home?
- Ⓐ 11:00
- Ⓑ 12:00
- Ⓒ 1:00
- Ⓓ 2:00

Tell time to the nearest half hour and relate time to events

Data Analysis and Probability

Toy Box or Toolbox?

Name _____

Cut and paste.
Put each thing in the correct box.

Toy Box	Toolbox

Sort objects and data by common attributes and describe the categories

©2003 by Evan-Moor Corp. • Basic Math Skills, Grade 1 • EMC 3014

Sort the Animals

Sort the animals into two groups.
Circle the animals in one group **red**.
Circle the animals in the other group **blue**.
Then tell about each group.

Red _____

_____

Blue _____

_____

Sort objects and data by common attributes and describe the categories

Data Analysis & Probability   EMC 3014 • Basic Math Skills, Grade 1 • ©2003 by Evan-Moor Corp.

Find My Things

Matt is getting dressed for school.
Amy is getting dressed for bed.
Draw a line from each thing to the correct child.

Sort objects and data by common attributes and describe the categories

What Does Not Belong?

Name _____

---

1. What does NOT belong? Make an **X** on it. Tell how the other things are alike.

_____

_____

2. What does NOT belong? Make an **X** on it. Tell how the other things are alike.

_____

_____

---

3. What does NOT belong? Make an **X** on it. Tell how the other things are alike.

_____

_____

4. What does NOT belong? Make an **X** on it. Tell how the other things are alike.

_____

_____

Sort objects and data by common attributes and describe the categories

Data Analysis & Probability   EMC 3014 • Basic Math Skills, Grade 1 • ©2003 by Evan-Moor Corp.

Make a Set

Name _____

Box 1	Box 2
_____	_____
_____	_____
_____	_____
_____	_____

1. Go to the Word Box.

2. Find 4 things that go together.

3. Write them in Box 1.

4. How are they alike?

1. Go to the Word Box.

2. Find 4 more things that go together.

3. Write them in Box 2.

4. How are they alike?

_____

_____

_____

_____

Word Box

tree	girl	hamster	car	rose
pencil	bed	boy	lamp	book
wagon	dog	goldfish	cow	table
chair	cat	mother	bicycle	teacher

Sort objects and data by common attributes and describe the categories

Data Analysis & Probability

Math Test

Fill in the circle next to the correct answer.

1. Which shape goes with this set?

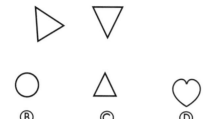

ⒶⒷⒸⒹ

2. Which shape goes with this set?

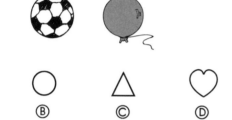

ⒶⒷⒸⒹ

3. Which thing goes with this set?

ⒶⒷⒸⒹ

4. Which thing goes in this box?

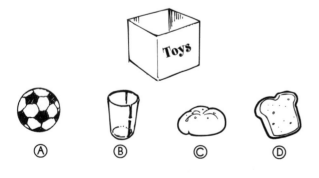

ⒶⒷⒸⒹ

5. Which thing does NOT go in this box?

ⒶⒷⒸⒹ

6. Which thing does NOT belong with the others?

ⒶⒷⒸⒹ

7. How are these things alike?

Ⓐ You can wear them.
Ⓑ You can eat them.
Ⓒ You can write with them.
Ⓓ You can buy things with them.

8. How are these things alike?

Ⓐ You can wear them.
Ⓑ You can eat them.
Ⓒ You can write with them.
Ⓓ You can buy things with them.

Sort objects and data by common attributes and describe the categories

Lost Teeth

Name _____

The children in Room 7 wrote their names on this graph when they lost a tooth. Look at the graph. Count the teeth.

September	Josh	Jerome		
October	Amy	Misha	Juan	Morgan
November	Carlos	Tim	Sasha	
December				

Fill in these blanks.

1. They lost the most teeth in the month of _____.

2. They lost the fewest teeth in the month of _____.

3. They lost _____ teeth in all.

Draw more teeth on the graph.
Show that Jen, Kai, and Eli lost a tooth in December.

Interpret data using pictures and graphs

I Like Ice Cream

Name _____

Mrs. Kim's class picked the ice-cream flavor they liked best. Look at the graph. Count the ice-cream cones.

vanilla	🍦🍦🍦🍦🍦🍦🍦🍦
chocolate	🍦🍦🍦🍦🍦🍦🍦🍦🍦🍦
strawberry	🍦🍦🍦

Answer the questions.

1. What flavors are shown on the graph?

_____   _____   _____

2. How many children picked each flavor?

_____   _____   _____

3. Draw a cone on the graph by the flavor you like best.

Interpret data using pictures and graphs

Data Analysis & Probability   EMC 3014 • Basic Math Skills, Grade 1 • ©2003 by Evan-Moor Corp.

Which Sport Do You Like Best?

Mr. Tran's class picked the sport they liked best.
Look at the chart. Count the tally marks.

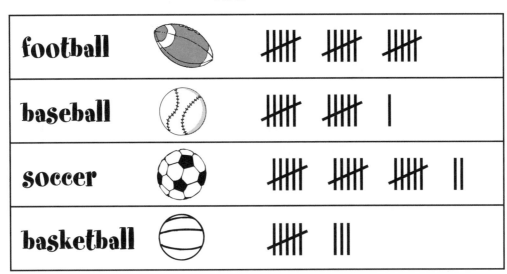

||||| = 5

Answer the questions.

1. Which sports are listed on the chart?

_____

2. Which sport was picked the most? _____

3. Which sport was picked the least? _____

4. How many children picked football? _____

5. Make a red tally mark by the sport you like best.

Interpret data using pictures and graphs

Our Favorite Pets

Name _____

The children in Room 12 voted for their favorite pet.
Look at the bar graph.

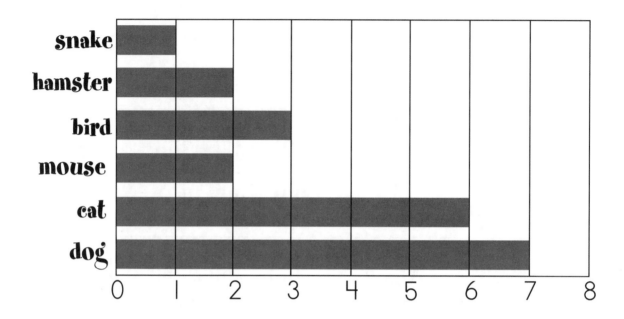

Answer the questions.

1. Which pet did they like best of all? _____

2. Which pet did they like least of all? _____

3. Which two pets got the same number of votes?

_____   _____

4. Color a box for the pet you like best.

Interpret data using pictures and graphs

          EMC 3014 • Basic Math Skills, Grade 1 • ©2003 by Evan-Moor Corp.

Which Color Do You Like Best?

Name _____

Finish the tally chart. Ask 10 boys and girls, "Which color do you like best?" Have them pick one of the colors. Make a tally mark by that color.

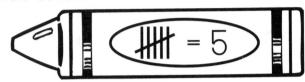

red	
blue	
green	
yellow	
orange	
purple	

Answer the questions.

1. Which color was picked the most? _____

2. Which color was picked the least? _____

3. Were any of the colors picked the same amount? _____
If so, which ones?

_____

Data Analysis & Probability

Math Test

Fill in the circle next to the correct answer.

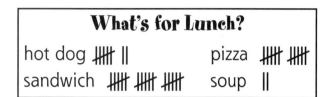

What's for Lunch?	
hot dog 卌 ‖	pizza 卌 卌
sandwich 卌 卌 卌	soup ‖

1. Look at the tally chart. What is it about?

- Ⓐ food
- Ⓑ games
- Ⓒ pets
- Ⓓ toys

2. Which food was picked by the most children?

- Ⓐ hot dog
- Ⓑ pizza
- Ⓒ sandwich
- Ⓓ soup

3. How many of the children had sandwiches for lunch?

- Ⓐ 7
- Ⓑ 10
- Ⓒ 12
- Ⓓ 15

4. How many more picked pizza than soup?

- Ⓐ 2   Ⓒ 8
- Ⓑ 4   Ⓓ 10

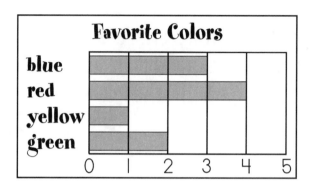

Favorite Colors

5. Look at the graph. What is it about

- Ⓐ numbers
- Ⓑ letters
- Ⓒ colors
- Ⓓ toys

6. Which color was picked the most?

- Ⓐ blue
- Ⓑ red
- Ⓒ yellow
- Ⓓ green

7. Which color was picked the least?

- Ⓐ blue
- Ⓑ red
- Ⓒ yellow
- Ⓓ green

8. How many more picked red than yellow?

- Ⓐ 1   Ⓒ 3
- Ⓑ 2   Ⓓ 4

Interpret data using pictures and graphs

Data Analysis & Probability

Sleeping in a Tent

Name _____

Ask 12 boys and girls, "Have you ever slept in a tent?"
Have the boys and girls write their names under **Yes** or **No**.

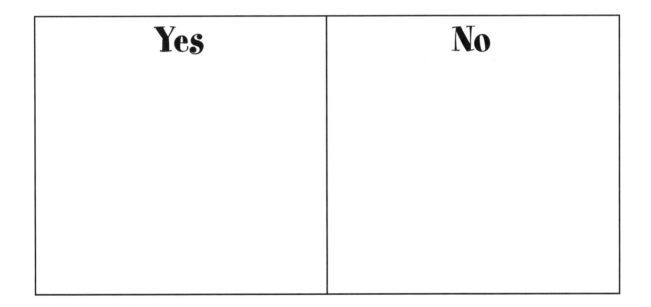

Yes	No

1. How many boys and girls have slept in a tent? _____

2. How many boys and girls have NOT slept in a tent? _____

3. Have you slept in a tent? Write your name in the correct box.

Represent and compare data using pictures, bar graphs, tally charts, and picture graphs

Data Analysis & Probability

Off to School We Go

Name _____

Ask 10 boys and girls, "How do you get to school?"
Have the boys and girls write their names under the correct picture.

1. How many boys and girls ride the bus? _____

2. How many boys and girls walk to school? _____

3. Which way do the most boys and girls get to school? _____

4. How do you get to school? Write your name in the correct box.

Represent and compare data by using pictures, bar graphs, tally charts, and picture graphs

         EMC 3014 • Basic Math Skills, Grade 1 • ©2003 by Evan-Moor Corp.

Farmer Frank's Fruit Stand

Name _____

Color the graph to show what Farmer Frank sold at his fruit stand.

8 boxes of cherries

7 baskets of berries

10 watermelons

5 pears

	1	2	3	4	5	6	7	8	9	10

1. How many boxes did you color for ? Why?

_____

2. How many more did Farmer Frank sell than ?

_____

3. Write one more question about the graph. Then write the answer.

_____

_____

Represent and compare data by using pictures, bar graphs, tally charts, and picture graphs

Pick a Lunch

Mr. Garcia is taking a lunch count.
Color the boxes to show how many
of each item he counted.

hamburger	𝍫𝍫𝍫 III
sandwich	III
pizza	𝍫𝍫𝍫 II
taco	𝍫𝍫𝍫
milk	𝍫𝍫𝍫 𝍫𝍫𝍫 𝍫𝍫𝍫
juice	𝍫𝍫𝍫 III

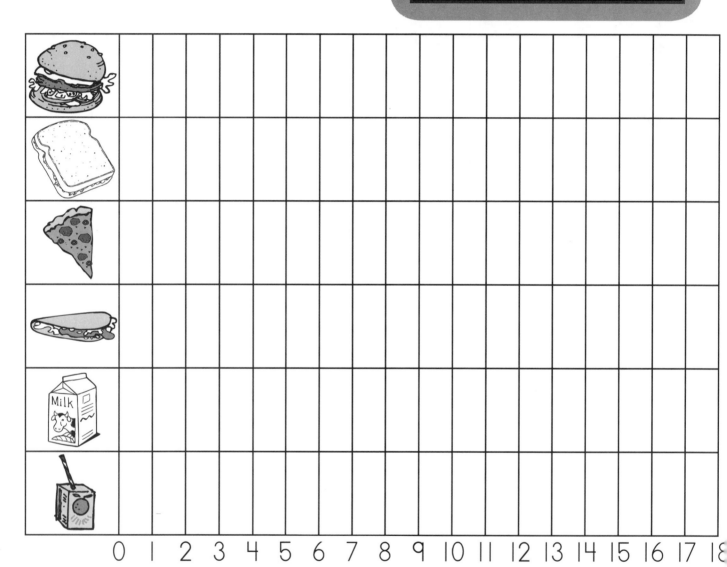

0 1 2 3 4 5 6 7 8 9 10 11 12 13 14 15 16 17 18

Write two things this graph shows you.

1. _____

2. _____

Represent and compare data by using pictures, bar graphs, tally charts, and picture graphs

How Many Letters?

Name _____

Write the names of 3 friends.
Count the number of letters in their names.

_____ George _____ ___ 6 ___ _____ _____

_____ _____ _____ _____

Write the names below the graph.
Color a box for each letter in each name.

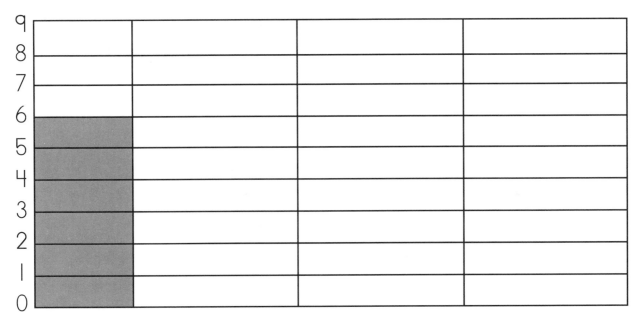

____ George ____ _____ _____ _____

Look at the colored boxes.

1. Who has the longest name? How do you know? _____

_____

2. Write two more things this graph shows you. _____

_____

_____

Represent and compare data by using pictures, bar graphs, tally charts, and picture graphs

Math Test

Fill in the circle next to the correct answer.

Our Favorite Fruit

apple ЖЖ ‖   banana ‖‖‖
orange ЖЖ   grapes ‖‖‖

1. Look at the tally chart. What is it about?

Ⓐ drinks

Ⓑ vegetables

Ⓒ fruits

Ⓓ snacks

2. How many people like grapes the best?

Ⓐ 5

Ⓑ 4

Ⓒ 3

Ⓓ 7

3. How many people like bananas the best?

Ⓐ 5

Ⓑ 4

Ⓒ 3

Ⓓ 7

4. Which fruit is liked best of all?

Ⓐ apple

Ⓑ orange

Ⓒ banana

Ⓓ grapes

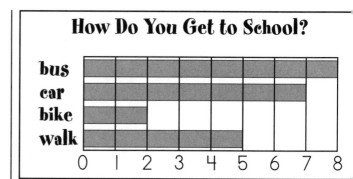

How Do You Get to School?

bus
car
bike
walk
0 1 2 3 4 5 6 7 8

5. Look at the graph. What is it about?

Ⓐ getting to the park

Ⓑ getting to the zoo

Ⓒ getting to the school

Ⓓ getting to the mall

6. How do most children get to school?

Ⓐ bus

Ⓑ car

Ⓒ bike

Ⓓ walk

7. How many children walk to school?

Ⓐ 8   Ⓑ 6   Ⓒ 5   Ⓓ 2

8. How many more children ride the bus than ride a bike?

Ⓐ 8   Ⓑ 6   Ⓒ 5   Ⓓ 2

Represent and compare data by using pictures, bar graphs, tally charts, and picture graphs

Resources

1	3	2	0	3	1	4	5
+0	+1	+3	+6	+3	+5	+2	+0
1	4	5	6	7	8		

4	2	1	2	3	2	6	0
+1	+1	+4	+0	+2	+4	+0	+0

2	5	0	0	1	0	1	1
+2	+1	+3	+1	+1	+4	+3	+2

- -

2	0	4	1	2	4	1	3
+2	+6	+1	+3	+0	+2	+0	+2

0	5	3	2	3	0	6	2
+5	+1	+3	+3	+1	+1	+0	+4

3	1	2	0	1	5	1	0
+0	+4	+1	+4	+2	+0	+1	+3

Name _____

Time: _____   **Number Correct:** _____

4	3	5	2	4	6	5	2
−3	−2	−4	−2	−0	−3	−2	−1

6	4	1	6	4	5	6	5
−2	−1	−0	−6	−2	−0	−5	−1

3	5	2	6	5	3	4	3
−1	−3	−0	−4	−5	−3	−4	−0

- -

Name _____

Time: _____   **Number Correct:** _____

5	6	3	6	3	4	6	5
−1	−2	−3	−5	−0	−2	−6	−0

2	5	6	4	1	2	5	3
−1	−2	−3	−0	−1	−2	−4	−2

6	5	4	3	2	6	5	4
−1	−3	−4	−1	−0	−4	−5	−3

Name _____

Time: _____   Number Correct: _____

3	2	1	4	5	2	0	4
$+1$	$+3$	-1	$+2$	-4	-2	$+6$	-0

6	2	1	4	5	4	0	2
-3	$+0$	$+4$	-2	-2	$+1$	$+1$	-1

2	6	5	4	6	6	3	2
$+2$	-2	$+1$	-1	-5	-6	-2	$+4$

- -

Name _____

Time: _____   Number Correct: _____

5	4	3	1	5	1	5	6
$+0$	-2	$+3$	$+5$	-3	$+0$	-5	-2

4	4	6	2	6	2	1	3
-4	$+1$	-3	$+1$	-4	$+4$	-0	$+2$

3	2	3	5	4	2	6	6
$+1$	-2	-3	-1	-3	$+3$	-5	-0

EMC 3014 • Basic Math Skills, Grade 1 • ©2003 by Evan-Moor Corp.

Name _____

Time: _____   Number Correct: _____

2	4	5	6	6	2	3	4
+5	+3	+5	+3	+1	+8	+4	+2

1	6	5	7	2	3	6	10
+9	+0	+4	+2	+7	+3	+2	+0

2	0	7	3	4	8	6	1
+6	+7	+3	+6	+5	+2	+4	+8

- -

Name _____

Time: _____   Number Correct: _____

4	2	3	5	4	2	8	6
+2	+5	+4	+5	+3	+8	+0	+1

6	1	4	3	2	5	7	10
+2	+9	+6	+5	+7	+4	+2	+0

1	2	3	0	8	7	4	3
+8	+6	+7	+7	+2	+3	+5	+6

Name _____

Time: _____   Number Correct: _____

6	8	9	7	8	6	10	10
−0	−5	−6	−5	−1	−6	−1	−10

8	6	7	9	9	7	10	10
−8	−5	−4	−7	−0	−1	−0	−8

10	8	7	8	9	10	8	9
−4	−7	−6	−2	−4	−3	−0	−2

- -

Name _____

Time: _____   Number Correct: _____

8	10	6	10	6	7	8	10
−4	−2	−2	−1	−5	−3	−3	−5

6	8	10	6	9	7	9	7
−1	−6	−7	−3	−5	−2	−8	−7

10	9	8	10	6	10	8	9
−4	−9	−2	−9	−4	−6	−7	−3

Name _____

Time: _____   Number Correct: _____

9 − 0	6 + 1	2 + 8	7 − 5	3 + 4	4 + 2	9 − 7	6 − 2
8 − 4	5 + 4	7 + 3	10 − 5	3 + 3	6 + 2	8 − 3	6 − 5
10 − 2	0 + 7	9 − 1	7 − 3	8 − 8	2 + 6	3 + 6	10 − 4

- -

Name _____

Time: _____   Number Correct: _____

9 − 4	2 + 5	2 + 6	10 − 10	10 − 3	5 + 5	6 − 0	3 + 7
8 + 0	8 − 5	6 − 4	8 + 2	6 + 4	8 − 7	9 − 3	6 + 3
10 − 0	4 + 3	9 − 6	1 + 9	8 − 2	4 + 5	1 + 6	10 − 6

©2003 by Evan-Moor Corp. • Basic Math Skills, Grade 1 • EMC 3014   **Timed Tests 249**

Name _____

Timed Test 13
Addition Facts 10–13

Time: _____   Number Correct: _____

2 +9	5 +8	7 +3	3 +9	5 +7	4 +9	5 +5	6 +4

4 +8	4 +6	1 +9	7 +5	9 +2	5 +6	2 +8	10 +3

6 +5	8 +2	4 +7	8 +3	9 +1	7 +6	8 +4	10 +2

- -

Name _____

Timed Test 14
Addition Facts 10–13

Time: _____   Number Correct: _____

5 +5	3 +8	9 +3	7 +4	8 +5	3 +7	6 +6	9 +4

8 +2	10 +1	6 +7	4 +9	9 +1	8 +3	6 +5	10 +3

5 +8	3 +9	7 +6	7 +3	5 +6	7 +5	1 +9	4 +8

250 Timed Tests

EMC 3014 • Basic Math Skills, Grade 1 • ©2003 by Evan-Moor Corp

Name _____

Time: _____   Number Correct: _____

12	11	10	13	11	12	11	10
− 3	− 5	− 7	− 9	− 4	− 6	− 2	− 10

13	12	10	11	13	10	11	12
− 10	− 4	− 5	− 9	− 3	− 3	− 6	− 7

10	11	12	13	11	12	10	13
− 9	− 7	− 8	− 5	− 3	− 5	− 8	− 6

- -

Name _____

Time: _____   Number Correct: _____

12	10	12	11	12	10	13	13
− 2	− 1	− 6	− 5	− 3	− 7	− 9	− 6

12	11	13	11	10	11	12	12
− 7	− 2	− 13	− 6	− 3	− 9	− 5	− 4

13	11	13	12	13	10	11	10
− 7	− 4	− 5	− 9	− 8	− 6	− 8	− 0

Name _____

Time: _____   Number Correct: _____

5 + 8	12 − 3	7 + 3	11 − 5	3 + 9	10 − 7	6 + 7	13 − 9
11 − 4	4 + 9	5 + 6	6 + 4	4 + 8	13 − 6	11 − 2	10 − 10
9 + 2	7 + 5	4 + 6	12 − 4	2 + 8	12 − 6	9 + 4	10 + 3

- -

Name _____

Time: _____   Number Correct: _____

10 − 9	11 − 7	2 + 9	12 − 8	7 + 4	13 − 5	6 + 6	3 + 7
8 + 5	9 + 3	11 − 3	5 + 7	12 − 7	7 + 6	12 − 5	13 − 8
11 − 6	12 − 9	6 + 5	13 − 7	11 − 8	11 − 9	9 + 2	8 + 4

EMC 3014 • Basic Math Skills, Grade 1 • ©2003 by Evan-Moor Corp.

Name _____

Time: _____   Number Correct: _____

2 +9	5 +8	2 +8	6 +7	4 +9	8 +6	9 +6	7 +7
4 +6	3 +9	9 +1	3 +8	7 +4	8 +7	6 +4	10 +5
5 +5	8 +4	5 +6	6 +8	7 +5	8 +3	9 +5	9 +3

- -

Name _____

Time: _____   Number Correct: _____

9 +4	8 +2	3 +9	8 +7	6 +4	3 +8	7 +4	10 +1
4 +7	5 +5	7 +8	4 +8	5 +7	8 +5	7 +6	6 +9
6 +8	5 +6	9 +3	7 +5	5 +8	6 +5	5 +9	4 +9

Name _____

Time: _____   **Number Correct:** _____

10 − 9	15 − 6	12 −3	11 − 7	10 − 8	12 − 6	15 − 8	12 − 9
14 − 5	15 − 9	12 − 8	11 − 3	10 − 7	13 − 8	12 −4	11 − 8
14 − 9	11 − 2	10 − 5	12 − 7	14 − 8	13 − 5	15 − 7	14 − 6

- -

Name _____

Time: _____   **Number Correct:** _____

12 − 5	15 − 5	10 −10	12 − 3	13 − 7	15 −15	14 − 0	11 −4
11 − 9	12 − 4	13 − 9	13 − 6	12 − 8	13 −13	11 − 6	14 − 7
15 − 7	14 − 9	12 − 9	11 − 7	13 − 8	11 − 2	14 − 8	12 − 7

     EMC 3014 • Basic Math Skills, Grade 1 • ©2003 by Evan-Moor Corp.

Name _____

Time: _____   Number Correct: _____

2 +8	9 +1	11 −9	5 +7	8 +4	13 −7	12 −8	7 +6
9 +6	7 +5	15 −6	13 −6	8 +7	10 −8	11 −7	8 +5
9 +3	14 −5	10 −9	7 +8	6 +8	10 −4	13 −4	5 +9

- -

Name _____

Time: _____   Number Correct: _____

6 +6	5 +8	11 −5	12 −9	4 +9	11 −6	6 +7	12 −7
8 +6	12 −6	6 +9	13 −8	5 +9	11 −3	9 +4	14 −7
15 −9	13 −9	7 +7	9 +5	14 −8	12 −4	7 +4	15 −7

7 +8	6 +5	3 +9	8 +9	6 +7	7 +9	8 +3	4 +9
6 +6	8 +4	5 +9	5 +7	3 +8	4 +7	9 +3	8 +5
5 +6	6 +9	8 +8	7 +4	8 +7	9 +8	9 +4	7 +7

- -

4 +8	7 +6	8 +6	6 +8	10 +8	8 +9	6 +7	2 +9
10 +7	9 +6	9 +2	8 +4	4 +7	8 +8	3 +8	8 +7
7 +7	5 +6	9 +7	6 +9	9 +8	7 +5	8 +5	9 +9

EMC 3014 • Basic Math Skills, Grade 1 • ©2003 by Evan-Moor Corp.

Name _____

Time: _____   Number Correct: _____

16	15	13	11	15	18	14	11
− 7	− 8	− 6	− 2	− 7	− 9	− 6	− 9

14	12	13	14	13	11	12	17
− 9	− 9	− 8	− 7	− 4	− 7	− 3	− 9

13	18	17	14	16	12	15	11
− 7	− 18	− 8	− 5	− 0	− 8	− 6	− 4

- -

Name _____

Time: _____   Number Correct: _____

17	14	14	13	12	11	13	12
− 7	− 8	− 9	− 5	− 7	− 6	− 9	− 5

16	14	13	17	15	16	11	12
− 9	− 5	− 7	− 8	− 6	− 8	− 5	− 8

13	12	16	14	14	13	12	15
− 13	− 9	− 7	− 4	− 6	− 6	− 4	− 9

Name _____

Time: _____   Number Correct: _____

11	7	9	12	8	4	11	11
-9	$+6$	$+7$	-7	$+6$	$+9$	-8	-3

6	13	16	6	15	8	12	10
$+5$	-7	-9	$+9$	-8	$+4$	-9	$+4$

8	12	13	6	3	5	13	12
$+8$	-4	-6	$+8$	$+9$	$+8$	-8	-6

- -

Name _____

Time: _____   Number Correct: _____

14	17	3	7	16	13	5	14
-7	-8	$+8$	$+8$	-16	-4	$+9$	-5

7	15	18	9	8	14	4	7
$+9$	-7	-9	$+8$	$+3$	-6	$+7$	$+7$

14	16	17	9	8	13	15	13
-9	-8	-9	$+6$	$+5$	-9	-6	-5

EMC 3014 • Basic Math Skills, Grade 1 • ©2003 by Evan-Moor Corp.

Math Timed Tests–Class Record Sheet

Student Names												
1 + 0–6												
2 + 0–6												
3 – 0–6												
4 – 0–6												
5 +/– 0–6												
6 +/– 0–6												
7 + 6–10												
8 + 6–10												
9 – 6–10												
10 – 6–10												
11 +/– 0–10												
12 +/– 0–10												
13 + 10–13												
14 + 10–13												
15 – 10–13												

Class Record Sheet

Math Timed Tests–Class Record Sheet

Student Names

16 – 10–13												
17 +/– 10–13												
18 +/– 10–13												
19 + 10–15												
20 + 10–15												
21 – 10–15												
22 – 10–15												
23 +/– 10–15												
24 +/– 10–15												
25 + 11–18												
26 + 11–18												
27 – 11–18												
28 – 11–18												
29 +/– 11–18												
30 +/– 11–18												

Class Record Sheet

EMC 3014 • Basic Math Skills, Grade 1 • ©2003 by Evan-Moor Corp.

Name _____

Math Test Page _____

1. Ⓐ Ⓑ Ⓒ Ⓓ   5. Ⓐ Ⓑ Ⓒ Ⓓ

2. Ⓐ Ⓑ Ⓒ Ⓓ   6. Ⓐ Ⓑ Ⓒ Ⓓ

3. Ⓐ Ⓑ Ⓒ Ⓓ   7. Ⓐ Ⓑ Ⓒ Ⓓ

4. Ⓐ Ⓑ Ⓒ Ⓓ   8. Ⓐ Ⓑ Ⓒ Ⓓ

Name _____

Math Test Page _____

1. Ⓐ Ⓑ Ⓒ Ⓓ   5. Ⓐ Ⓑ Ⓒ Ⓓ

2. Ⓐ Ⓑ Ⓒ Ⓓ   6. Ⓐ Ⓑ Ⓒ Ⓓ

3. Ⓐ Ⓑ Ⓒ Ⓓ   7. Ⓐ Ⓑ Ⓒ Ⓓ

4. Ⓐ Ⓑ Ⓒ Ⓓ   8. Ⓐ Ⓑ Ⓒ Ⓓ

Name _____

Math Test Page _____

1. Ⓐ Ⓑ Ⓒ Ⓓ   5. Ⓐ Ⓑ Ⓒ Ⓓ

2. Ⓐ Ⓑ Ⓒ Ⓓ   6. Ⓐ Ⓑ Ⓒ Ⓓ

3. Ⓐ Ⓑ Ⓒ Ⓓ   7. Ⓐ Ⓑ Ⓒ Ⓓ

4. Ⓐ Ⓑ Ⓒ Ⓓ   8. Ⓐ Ⓑ Ⓒ Ⓓ

Name _____

Math Test Page _____

1. Ⓐ Ⓑ Ⓒ Ⓓ   5. Ⓐ Ⓑ Ⓒ Ⓓ

2. Ⓐ Ⓑ Ⓒ Ⓓ   6. Ⓐ Ⓑ Ⓒ Ⓓ

3. Ⓐ Ⓑ Ⓒ Ⓓ   7. Ⓐ Ⓑ Ⓒ Ⓓ

4. Ⓐ Ⓑ Ⓒ Ⓓ   8. Ⓐ Ⓑ Ⓒ Ⓓ

Awards

You
Did It!

_____
name

_____
task

MATH
Super Star

_____

Good Job!

Hip Hop Hooray!

_____

You're doing better!

_____

is ready for
the next
timed test.

EMC 3014 • Basic Math Skills, Grade 1 • ©2003 by Evan-Moor Corp.

0 +0	0 +3	0 +7	1 +0
1 +1	1 +2	1 +3	1 +6
1 +9	2 +0	2 +1	2 +2

©2003 by Evan-Moor Corp. • EMC 3014 (repeated on each card)

$\begin{array}{r} 2 \\ +3 \\ \hline \end{array}$	$\begin{array}{r} 2 \\ +4 \\ \hline \end{array}$	$\begin{array}{r} 2 \\ +5 \\ \hline \end{array}$	$\begin{array}{r} 2 \\ +6 \\ \hline \end{array}$
$\begin{array}{r} 2 \\ +7 \\ \hline \end{array}$	$\begin{array}{r} 2 \\ +8 \\ \hline \end{array}$	$\begin{array}{r} 2 \\ +9 \\ \hline \end{array}$	$\begin{array}{r} 3 \\ +1 \\ \hline \end{array}$
$\begin{array}{r} 3 \\ +2 \\ \hline \end{array}$	$\begin{array}{r} 3 \\ +3 \\ \hline \end{array}$	$\begin{array}{r} 3 \\ +4 \\ \hline \end{array}$	$\begin{array}{r} 3 \\ +5 \\ \hline \end{array}$

EMC 3014 • Basic Math Skills, Grade 1 • ©2003 by Evan-Moor Corp

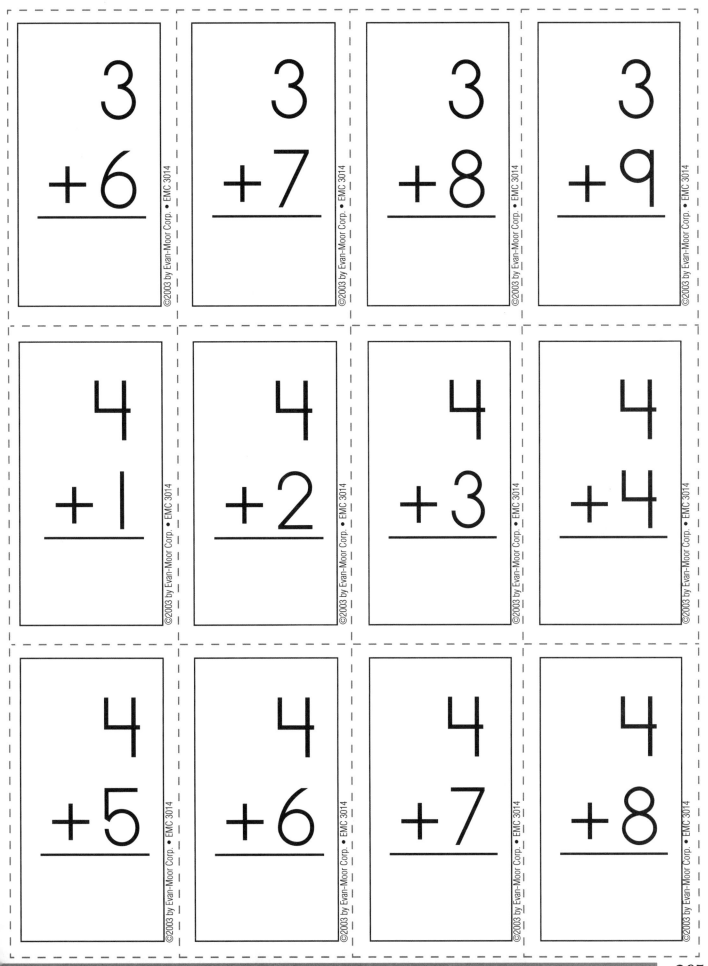

4 $+9$	5 $+0$	5 $+1$	5 $+2$
5 $+3$	5 $+4$	5 $+5$	5 $+6$
5 $+7$	5 $+8$	5 $+9$	6 $+1$

$$\begin{array}{r} 6 \\ +2 \\ \hline \end{array}$$

$$\begin{array}{r} 6 \\ +3 \\ \hline \end{array}$$

$$\begin{array}{r} 6 \\ +4 \\ \hline \end{array}$$

$$\begin{array}{r} 6 \\ +5 \\ \hline \end{array}$$

$$\begin{array}{r} 6 \\ +6 \\ \hline \end{array}$$

$$\begin{array}{r} 6 \\ +7 \\ \hline \end{array}$$

$$\begin{array}{r} 6 \\ +8 \\ \hline \end{array}$$

$$\begin{array}{r} 6 \\ +9 \\ \hline \end{array}$$

$$\begin{array}{r} 7 \\ +0 \\ \hline \end{array}$$

$$\begin{array}{r} 7 \\ +1 \\ \hline \end{array}$$

$$\begin{array}{r} 7 \\ +2 \\ \hline \end{array}$$

$$\begin{array}{r} 7 \\ +3 \\ \hline \end{array}$$

$$7 \atop +4$$

$$7 \atop +5$$

$$7 \atop +6$$

$$7 \atop +7$$

©2003 by Evan-Moor Corp. • EMC 3014

©2003 by Evan-Moor Corp. • EMC 3014

©2003 by Evan-Moor Corp. • EMC 3014

©2003 by Evan-Moor Corp. • EMC 3014

$$7 \atop +8$$

$$7 \atop +9$$

$$8 \atop +1$$

$$8 \atop +2$$

©2003 by Evan-Moor Corp. • EMC 3014

©2003 by Evan-Moor Corp. • EMC 3014

©2003 by Evan-Moor Corp. • EMC 3014

©2003 by Evan-Moor Corp. • EMC 3014

$$8 \atop +3$$

$$8 \atop +4$$

$$8 \atop +5$$

$$8 \atop +6$$

©2003 by Evan-Moor Corp. • EMC 3014

©2003 by Evan-Moor Corp. • EMC 3014

©2003 by Evan-Moor Corp. • EMC 3014

©2003 by Evan-Moor Corp. • EMC 3014

$$8 \atop +7$$

$$8 \atop +8$$

$$8 \atop +9$$

$$9 \atop +1$$

$$9 \atop +0$$

$$9 \atop +2$$

$$9 \atop +3$$

$$9 \atop +4$$

$$9 \atop +5$$

$$9 \atop +6$$

$$9 \atop +7$$

$$9 \atop +8$$

$$\begin{array}{r} 9 \\ + 9 \\ \hline \end{array}$$

$$\begin{array}{r} 10 \\ + 0 \\ \hline \end{array}$$

$$\begin{array}{r} 10 \\ + 1 \\ \hline \end{array}$$

$$\begin{array}{r} 10 \\ + 2 \\ \hline \end{array}$$

$$\begin{array}{r} 10 \\ + 3 \\ \hline \end{array}$$

$$\begin{array}{r} 10 \\ + 4 \\ \hline \end{array}$$

$$\begin{array}{r} 10 \\ + 5 \\ \hline \end{array}$$

$$\begin{array}{r} 10 \\ + 6 \\ \hline \end{array}$$

$$\begin{array}{r} 10 \\ + 7 \\ \hline \end{array}$$

$$\begin{array}{r} 10 \\ + 8 \\ \hline \end{array}$$

$$\begin{array}{r} 10 \\ + 9 \\ \hline \end{array}$$

$$\begin{array}{r} 10 \\ + 10 \\ \hline \end{array}$$

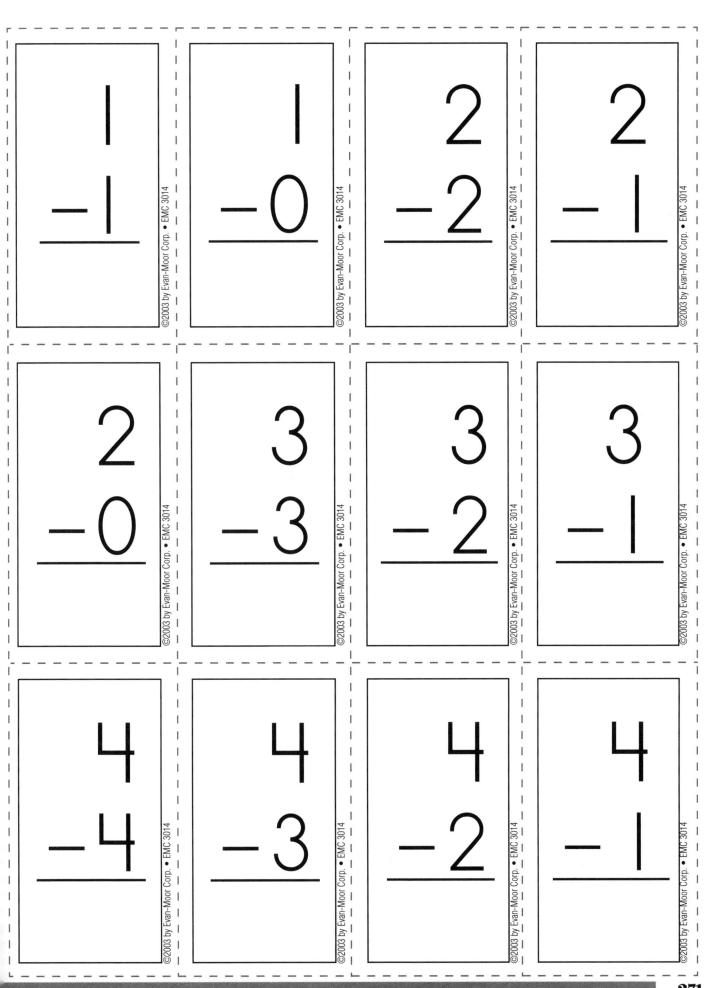

$$\begin{array}{r} 5 \\ -5 \\ \hline \end{array}$$

$$\begin{array}{r} 5 \\ -4 \\ \hline \end{array}$$

$$\begin{array}{r} 5 \\ -3 \\ \hline \end{array}$$

$$\begin{array}{r} 5 \\ -2 \\ \hline \end{array}$$

$$\begin{array}{r} 5 \\ -1 \\ \hline \end{array}$$

$$\begin{array}{r} 6 \\ -6 \\ \hline \end{array}$$

$$\begin{array}{r} 6 \\ -5 \\ \hline \end{array}$$

$$\begin{array}{r} 6 \\ -4 \\ \hline \end{array}$$

$$\begin{array}{r} 6 \\ -3 \\ \hline \end{array}$$

$$\begin{array}{r} 6 \\ -2 \\ \hline \end{array}$$

$$\begin{array}{r} 6 \\ -1 \\ \hline \end{array}$$

$$\begin{array}{r} 7 \\ -6 \\ \hline \end{array}$$

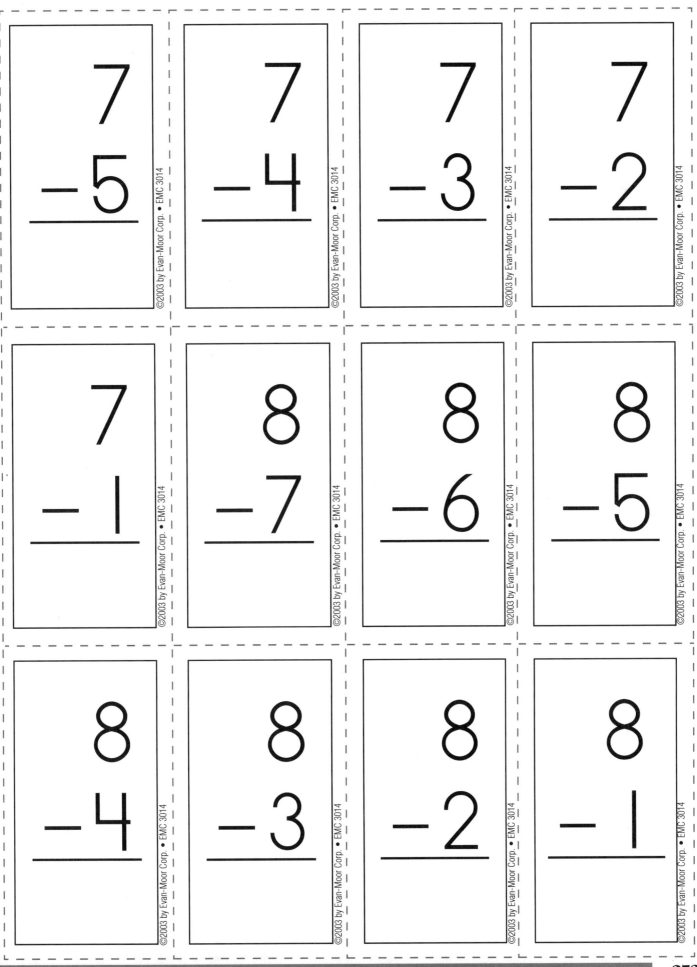

$\begin{array}{r} 9 \\ -8 \\ \hline \end{array}$	$\begin{array}{r} 9 \\ -7 \\ \hline \end{array}$	$\begin{array}{r} 9 \\ -6 \\ \hline \end{array}$	$\begin{array}{r} 9 \\ -5 \\ \hline \end{array}$
$\begin{array}{r} 9 \\ -4 \\ \hline \end{array}$	$\begin{array}{r} 9 \\ -3 \\ \hline \end{array}$	$\begin{array}{r} 9 \\ -2 \\ \hline \end{array}$	$\begin{array}{r} 9 \\ -1 \\ \hline \end{array}$
$\begin{array}{r} 10 \\ -9 \\ \hline \end{array}$	$\begin{array}{r} 10 \\ -8 \\ \hline \end{array}$	$\begin{array}{r} 10 \\ -7 \\ \hline \end{array}$	$\begin{array}{r} 10 \\ -6 \\ \hline \end{array}$

EMC 3014 • Basic Math Skills, Grade 1 • ©2003 by Evan-Moor Corp.

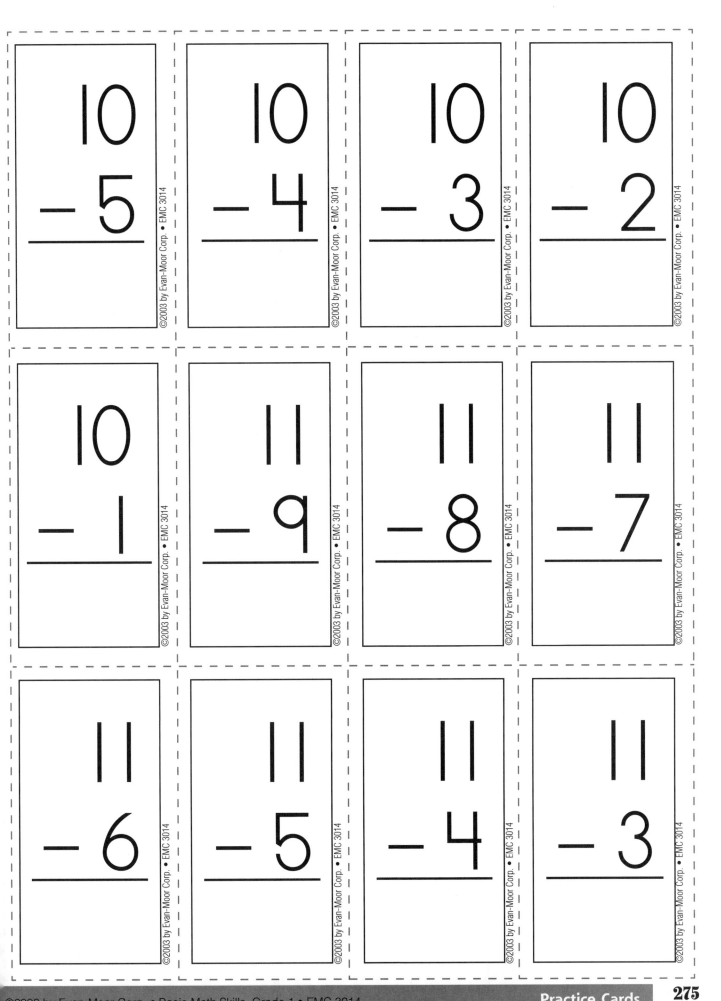

11	12	12	12
− 2	− 9	− 8	− 7

12	12	12	12
− 6	− 5	− 4	− 3

12	13	13	13
− 2	− 9	− 8	− 7

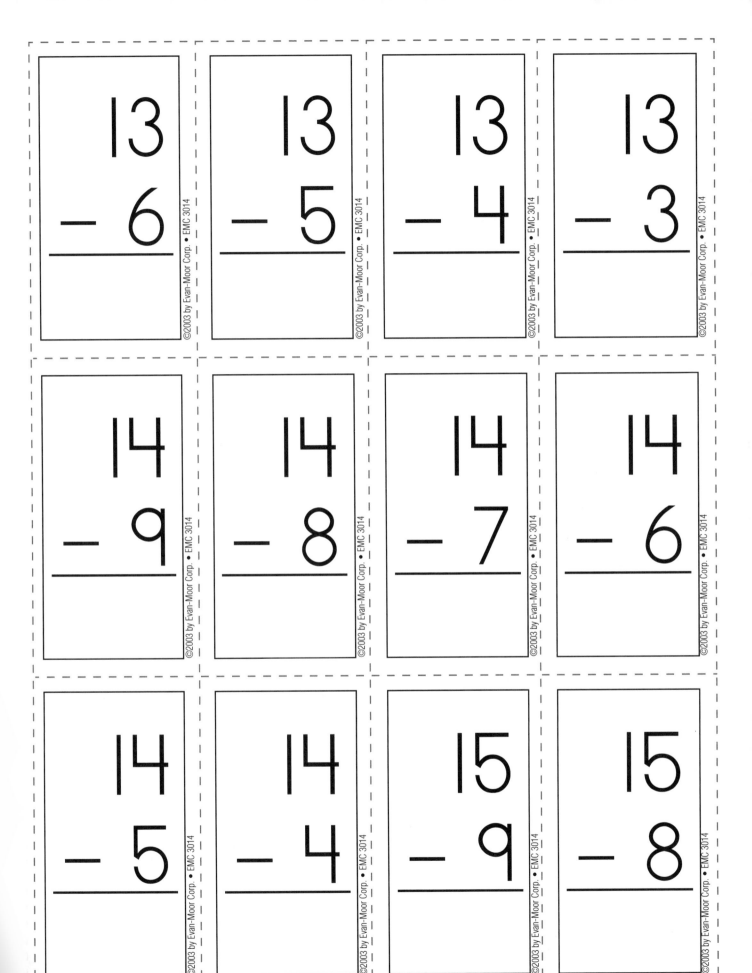

$\begin{array}{r} 15 \\ -\ 7 \\ \hline \end{array}$	$\begin{array}{r} 15 \\ -\ 6 \\ \hline \end{array}$	$\begin{array}{r} 16 \\ -\ 9 \\ \hline \end{array}$	$\begin{array}{r} 16 \\ -\ 8 \\ \hline \end{array}$
$\begin{array}{r} 16 \\ -\ 7 \\ \hline \end{array}$	$\begin{array}{r} 17 \\ -\ 9 \\ \hline \end{array}$	$\begin{array}{r} 17 \\ -\ 8 \\ \hline \end{array}$	$\begin{array}{r} 17 \\ -\ 7 \\ \hline \end{array}$
$\begin{array}{r} 18 \\ -\ 9 \\ \hline \end{array}$	$\begin{array}{r} 18 \\ -\ 8 \\ \hline \end{array}$	$\begin{array}{r} 19 \\ -\ 9 \\ \hline \end{array}$	$\begin{array}{r} 20 \\ -10 \\ \hline \end{array}$

Answer Key

Page 5

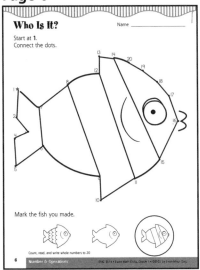

Page 6

Page 7

2 5 6 8 10
11 13 14 17 19 20

1 2 3 4 5 6 7 8 9 10
11 12 13 14 15 16 17 18 19 20

Circled pots will vary, but should equal 20.

Page 8

in-between

8 <u>9</u> 10
3 <u>4</u> 5
12 <u>13</u> 14
6 <u>7</u> 8
10 <u>11</u> 12
18 <u>19</u> 20
15 <u>16</u> 17
12 <u>13</u> 14

one more

6 <u>7</u>
11 <u>12</u>
9 <u>10</u>
15 <u>16</u>
7 <u>8</u>
4 <u>5</u>
19 <u>20</u>
14 <u>15</u>

one less

<u>2</u> 3
<u>8</u> 9
<u>10</u> 11
<u>19</u> 20
<u>12</u> 13
<u>6</u> 7
<u>16</u> 17
<u>11</u> 12

Page 9

2 5 7
8 10 12 13 14
16 18 19 20

Page 10

1. C   5. B
2. B   6. C
3. C   7. A
4. B   8. D

Page 11

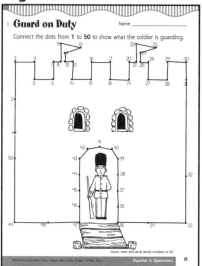

Page 12

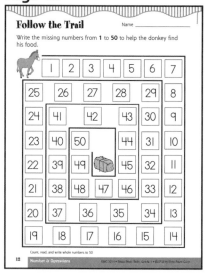

Page 13

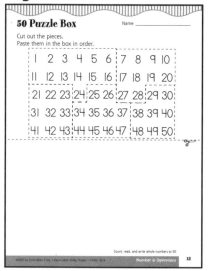

Page 14

in-between

1 <u>2</u> 3

11 <u>12</u> 13

37 <u>38</u> 39

19 <u>20</u> 21

48 <u>49</u> 50

25 <u>26</u> 27

44 <u>45</u> 46

32 <u>33</u> 34

one more

9 <u>10</u>

19 <u>20</u>

29 <u>30</u>

39 <u>40</u>

49 <u>50</u>

16 <u>17</u>

27 <u>28</u>

31 <u>32</u>

one less

<u>9</u> 10

<u>29</u> 30

<u>49</u> 50

<u>26</u> 27

<u>42</u> 43

<u>8</u> 9

<u>45</u> 46

<u>31</u> 32

Page 15

Answers will vary.

Page 16

1. A   5. D

2. C   6. A

3. D   7. D

4. C   8. A

Page 17

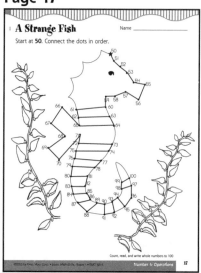

EMC 3014 • Basic Math Skills, Grade 1 • ©2003 by Evan-Moor Corr

Page 18

I Want to Go Home!   Name _____

Help Baby Bear to his den.
Color the boxes green that count from **70** to **100**.

70	71	60	43	29	74	52	80
44	72	19	40	61	12	49	67
30	73	74	75	20	16	62	53
68	36	79	76	77	78	79	80
90	89	88	63	68	51	43	81
91	39	87	86	85	84	83	82
92	93	12	64	54	42	65	14
50	94	95	96	97	98	99	100

Count, read, and write whole numbers to 100

18   Number & Operations

Page 19

Count to 100   Name _____

Write numbers **1** to **100** in order.

1	2	3	4	5	6	7	8	9	10
11	12	13	14	15	16	17	18	19	20
21	22	23	24	25	26	27	28	29	30
31	32	33	34	35	36	37	38	39	40
41	42	43	44	45	46	47	48	49	50
51	52	53	54	55	56	57	58	59	60
61	62	63	64	65	66	67	68	69	70
71	72	73	74	75	76	77	78	79	80
81	82	83	84	85	86	87	88	89	90
91	92	93	94	95	96	97	98	99	100

Count, read, and write whole numbers to 100

Number & Operations   19

Page 20

one more

5 7
11 12
20 21
36 37
10 11
42 43
24 25
49 50

one less

2 3
20 21
11 12
34 35
69 70
85 86
66 67
99 100

Page 20 continued

ten more

6 16
12 22
19 29
37 47
7 17
30 40
46 56
14 24

ten less

7 17
19 29
46 56
72 82
30 40
25 35
81 91
67 77

Page 21

Maria has 80 pennies.
Kelly has 100 pennies.
Tony has 74 pennies.
Kelly has the most.

Page 22

1. C   5. A
2. D   6. C
3. D   7. A
4. C   8. C

Page 23

1. 12
2. 100
3. 4
4. Accept answers close to 6 books.
5. Accept answers close to 9 books.

Page 24

1. 40
2. 10
3. 12
4. 24

Page 25

1. 15   4. 15
2. 20   5. 60
3. 50   6. 30

Page 26

1. more than 30
2. less than 8
3. more than 9
4. less than 20

Page 27
Accept reasonable answers.

Page 28
1. C	5. A
2. C	6. B
3. B	7. A
4. C	8. B

Page 29
1. 1 < 3	4. 4 < 6
2. 6 > 2	5. 4 > 2
3. 5 < 7	6. 3 < 5

Page 30

Page 31
1. 8 > 6	14 <19	26 = 26
2. 43 > 40	15 < 51	90 > 89
3. 37 < 73	21 >12	48 > 44
4. 100 > 99	71 < 74	77 = 77

5. Answers will vary, but should be greater than 25.
6. Answers will vary, but should be less than 52.
7. 99

Page 32
1–12. Answers will vary.

1. <
2. >
3. >
4. <

Page 33
1. Ali won.   18 points > 16 points
2. Jamal won. 15 marbles < 27 marbles
3. Tom won.   8 fish < 11 fish
4. Meg won.   53 boxes > 35 boxes
5. Word problems will vary, but should refer to the difference in the scores.

Page 34
1. D	5. C
2. C	6. D
3. A	7. A
4. B	8. C

Page 35
1. 1 full cage, 4 rabbits left
2. 2 full cages, 2 rabbits left
3. 2 full cages, 0 rabbits left

Page 36
1. 1 ten 4 ones, 14 kittens
2. 2 tens 2 ones, 22 kittens
3. 4 tens 1 one, 41 kittens
4. 1 ten 3 ones, 13 kittens

Page 37
1. 4 tens 3 ones, 43 in all
2. 8 tens 8 ones, 88 in all
3. 2 tens 6 ones, 26 in all
4. 3 tens 2 ones, 32 in all
5. 6 tens 4 ones, 64 in all
6. 1 ten 0 ones, 10 in all

Page 38
2 tens 3 ones, 23 in all
4 tens 6 ones, 46 in all
5 tens 4 ones, 54 in all
2 tens 4 ones, 24 in all
4 tens 0 ones, 40 in all
3 tens 9 ones, 39 in all
Table: 55, 97, 63

Page 39
1. 1 ten 1 one, 11¢
2. 5 tens 6 ones, 56¢
3. 4 tens 5 ones, 45¢
4. 7 tens 9 ones, 79¢
5. 2 tens 4 ones, 24¢
6. 6 tens 8 ones, 68¢

Page 40
1. D	5. D
2. C	6. B
3. C	7. D
4. C	8. A

Page 41

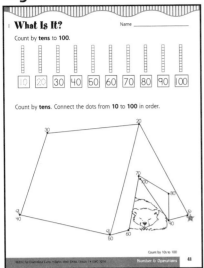

Page 42

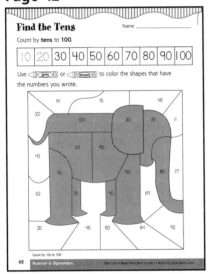

Page 43

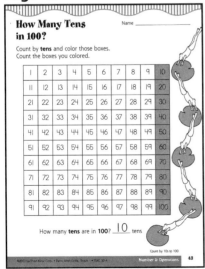

Page 44

Page 45

1. 40   4. 30
2. 90   5. 60
3. 80   6. 70

Page 46

1. C   5. A
2. A   6. D
3. D   7. C
4. C   8. B

Page 47

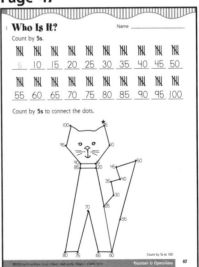

Page 48

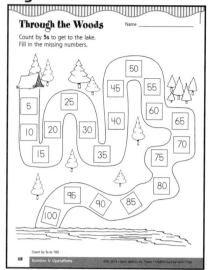

Page 49

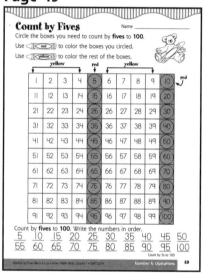

Page 50

5 10 15 20 25 30 35 40 45 50
55 60 65 70 75 80 85 90 95 100
100¢

5 10 15 20
40 45 50 55
85 90 95 100

Page 51

1. 25 nuts
2. 15 flowers
3. 35¢
4. 40 fish

Page 52

1. C   5. B
2. D   6. D
3. B   7. B
4. D   8. C

Page 53

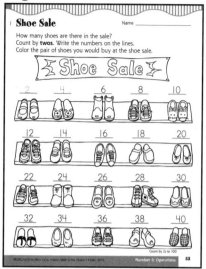

Page 54

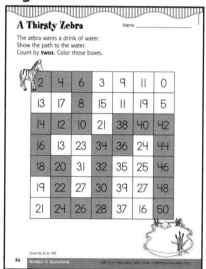

Page 55

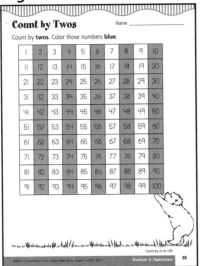

Page 56

2 <u>4</u> 6 <u>8</u> 10
12 <u>14</u> <u>16</u> <u>18</u> 20
22 <u>24</u> <u>26</u> 28 <u>30</u>
32 <u>34</u> 36 <u>38</u> <u>40</u>
42 <u>44</u> <u>46</u> <u>48</u> 50
52 <u>54</u> 56 <u>58</u> <u>60</u>
62 <u>64</u> <u>66</u> 68 <u>70</u>
72 <u>74</u> <u>76</u> <u>78</u> 80
82 <u>84</u> <u>86</u> 88 <u>90</u>
92 <u>94</u> <u>96</u> <u>98</u> <u>100</u>

Page 57

Circles will vary, but should each contain two items.
1. 20 mittens in all
2. 26 socks in all
3. 18 shoes in all
4. Answers will vary.

Page 58

1. C   5. D
2. B   6. D
3. A   7. C
4. B   8. A

Page 59

Page 60

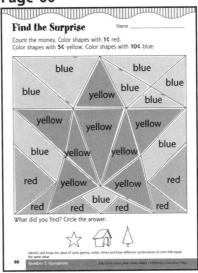

Page 61

1. 13¢   5. 22¢
2. 13¢   6. 26¢
3. 17¢   7. 30¢
4. 40¢   8. 41¢

Page 62

Answers will vary, but should equal the stated amount of money.

Page 63

1. <circle around 1 nickel and 5 pennies> 10¢
2. <circle around 2 nickels>   10¢
3. <circle around 1 dime and 1 nickel> 15¢
4. <circle around 1 dime, 1 nickel, and 5 pennies> 20¢
5. <circle around 3 dimes and 1 nickel> 35¢
6. <circle around 1 dime, 2 nickels, and 5 pennies> 25¢

Page 64

1. D   5. D
2. C   6. C
3. A   7. C
4. A   8. D

Page 65

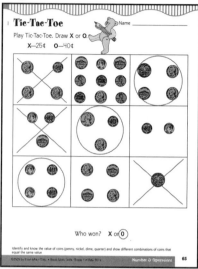

Page 66

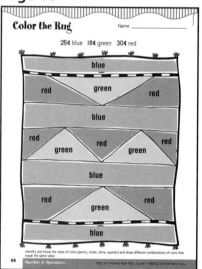

Page 67

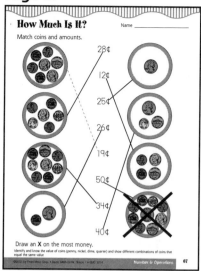

Page 68

1. 48¢ yes
2. 16¢ no
3. 45¢ yes
4. 30¢ yes
5. 65¢ no
6. 50¢ yes

Page 69

1. 15¢
2. 30¢
3. 40¢
4. 50¢
5. 60¢
6. Answers will vary.

Page 70

1. B   5. D
2. D   6. D
3. D   7. C
4. B   8. A

Page 71

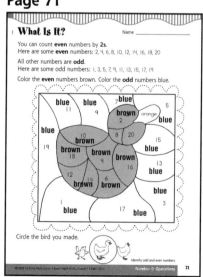

EMC 3014 • Basic Math Skills, Grade 1 • ©2003 by Evan-Moor Corp.

Page 72

Page 73
Circles will vary, but should contain two objects.
1. kites—even
2. wagons—odd
3. marbles—even
4. tops—even
5. skates—even
6. yo-yos—odd

Page 74
boxes around 1 3 5 7 9
circles around 0 2 4 6 8 10
1. 2 knocked down, even
2. 5 knocked down, odd
3. 1 knocked down, odd
4. 8 knocked down, even

Page 75
Jamal's Team—Lee, Josh, Jamal, Lupe, Kesha
Kim's Team—Pete, Ann, Kim, Susan, Carl, Anna

Page 76
1. A   5. C
2. B   6. B
3. B   7. C
4. C   8. D

Page 77

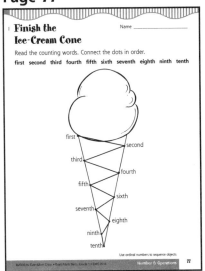

Page 78
first: Amy   fifth: Joy
sixth: Will   seventh: Aiko
third: Kay   second: Ken
fourth: Lea   ninth: Tim
eighth: Josh   tenth: Alex

Page 79

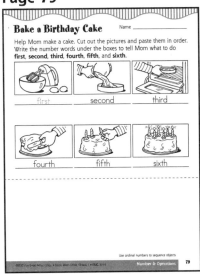

Page 80
1. goat
2. mouse
3. dog
4. 1st or first
5. 5th or fifth
6. 2nd or second
7. 7th or seventh
8. **X** on 3rd duckling; a circle around the 5th duckling

Page 81
Answers will vary.

Page 82
1. B   5. D
2. D   6. D
3. A   7. C
4. B   8. C

Page 83
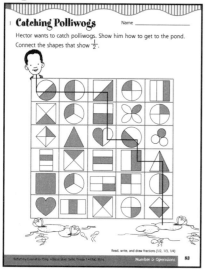

Page 84
1. & 3. Answers will vary, but should show two equal parts with one-half shaded.
2. & 4. Answers will vary, but should show four equal parts with one-fourth shaded.

Page 85
1. 1/2   2. 1/4   3. 1/2
4. 1/3   5. 1/3   6. 1/4
7. 1/4   8. 1/2   9. 1/2

Page 86
1. pizza, apple circled
2. pizza, graham cracker circled
3. pizza, pie, graham cracker circled
4. 1/4

Page 87
1. sandwich should have a half colored
2. snack bar should have a third colored
3. orange should have a half colored
4. cookie should have a half colored
5. Answers will vary.

Page 88
1. D   5. B
2. C   6. C
3. C   7. B
4. D   8. A

Page 89
1. red—1, blue—1
2. red—1, blue—3
3. red—2, blue—1
4. red—4, blue—4

Page 90
Show these shaded:
1 tree, 2 bananas, 3 flowers
1 balloon, 2 hearts, 3 flowers
1 spider, 2 snails, 3 fish

Page 91
1. 1 apple circled
2. 2 apples circled
3. 1 cookie circled
4. 2 cookies circled
5. 1 nut circled
6. 3 nuts circled

Page 92
Show these circled:
1/2   1/4   1/3

1/3   1/2   1/3

1/4   1/2   1/4

Page 93
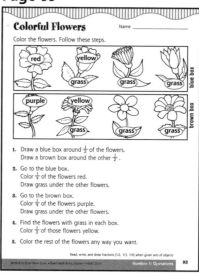

Page 94
1. C   5. C
2. B   6. D
3. A   7. B
4. D   8. B

Page 95
5 − 1 = 4
4 − 1 = 3
3 − 1 = 2
2 − 1 = 1
1 − 1 = 0

Page 96

$1 + 1 = 2$
$2 + 1 = 3$
$3 + 1 = 4$
$4 + 1 = 5$
$5 + 2 = 7$

Page 97

1. $4 + 1 = 5$
2. $4 - 1 = 3$
3. $7 - 5 = 2$
4. $4 + 4 = 8$
5. $10 - 6 = 4$
6. $3 + 6 = 9$
7. $8 + 2 = 10$
8. $9 - 8 = 1$

Pictures will vary, but should represent $5 - 2 = 3$.
Pictures will vary, but should represent $2 + 3 = 5$.

Page 98

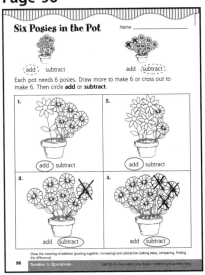

Page 99

$2 + 4 = 6$ $3 - 2 = 1$ $7 - 3 = 4$
$2 + 1 = 3$ $5 + 4 = 9$ $4 - 1 = 3$

Page 100

1. C   5. C
2. B   6. B
3. A   7. B
4. C   8. C

Page 101

2 4 3 1 5 0 1 1
honeybee

Page 102

Page 103

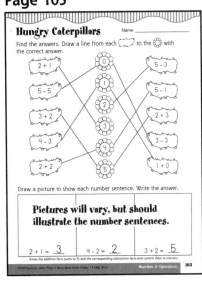

Page 104

Show X'd out:
1. $1 - 1$; $2 + 1$
2. $3 + 1$; $1 - 1$
3. $4 + 1$; $3 - 3$
4. $2 + 3$; $2 - 2$; $4 + 1$

Page 105

1. 5 oranges
2. 2 cherries
3. 2 lemons
4. 3 apples
5. 5 nuts
6. 4 baskets
7. Answers will vary.

Page 106
1. B 5. C
2. D 6. B
3. C 7. C
4. A 8. B

Page 107

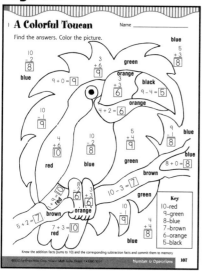

Page 108
9 4 3   5 2 1 10 9 8   4 1 6 3   3 1 7 8
the   plants   have   ears

Page 109
Answers will vary, but should equal 10.

7	4	(10)	5	3	2	8	2
9	(10)	9	3	5	9	9	(10)
4	7	6	7	6	(10)	7	(10)

Page 110

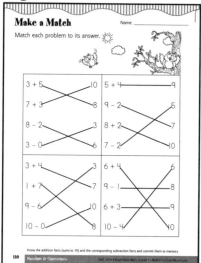

Page 111
1. 5 − 3 = 2
2. 6 + 4 = 10
3. 8 − 4 = 4
4. Answers will vary, but should reflect the picture.

Page 112
1. A 5. D
2. C 6. C
3. D 7. D
4. C 8. B

Page 113

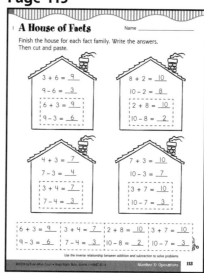

Page 114

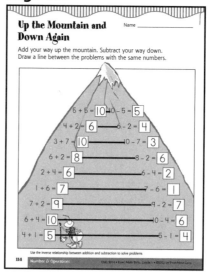

Page 115

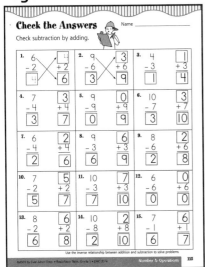

Page 116

5 + 2 = 7	6 + 4 = 10
2 + 5 = 7	4 + 6 = 10
7 − 5 = 2	10 − 6 = 4
7 − 2 = 5	10 − 4 = 6
8 + 1 = 9	3 + 5 = 8
1 + 8 = 9	5 + 3 = 8
9 − 8 = 1	8 − 3 = 5
9 − 1 = 8	8 − 5 = 3
4 + 3 = 7	5 + 4 = 9
3 + 4 = 7	4 + 5 = 9
7 − 4 = 3	9 − 5 = 4
7 − 3 = 4	9 − 4 = 5

Page 117

9 + 6 = 15	so	15 − 9 = 6
2 + 5 = 7	so	7 − 2 = 5
4 + 6 = 10	so	10 − 4 = 6
5 + 3 = 8	so	8 − 5 = 3
3 + 4 = 7	so	7 − 3 = 4
2 + 5 = 7	so	7 − 2 = 5
4 + 5 = 9	so	9 − 4 = 5
3 + 6 = 9	so	9 − 3 = 6
2 + 6 = 8	so	8 − 2 = 6
4 + 2 = 6	so	6 − 4 = 2
10 − 9 = 1	so	9 + 1 = 9
8 − 3 = 5	so	3 + 5 = 8
10 − 4 = 6	so	4 + 6 = 10
8 − 4 = 4	so	4 + 4 = 8
9 − 3 = 6	so	3 + 6 = 9
7 − 2 = 5	so	2 + 5 = 7
9 − 4 = 5	so	4 + 5 = 9
8 − 2 = 6	so	2 + 6 = 8
10 − 5 = 5	so	5 + 5 = 10
10 − 3 = 7	so	3 + 7 = 10

Page 118

1. C	5. B
2. D	6. D
3. A	7. C
4. B	8. D

Page 119

Page 120

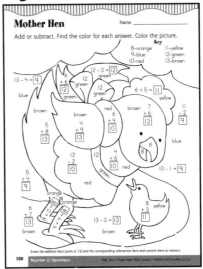

Page 121

1. 12 3 7 13 13 5
2. 9 5 11 4 11 13
3. 6 12 13 7 3 13
4. 13 8 5 12 2 9

Page 122

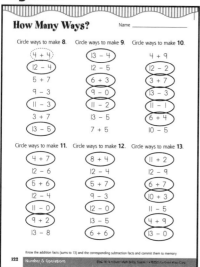

Page 123

1. 7 + 5 = 12
2. 13 − 9 = 4
3. 12 − 7 = 5
4. 6 + 6 = 12
5. Answers will vary, but should represent the picture.

Page 124

1. C   5. B
2. B   6. A
3. D   7. D
4. C   8. B

Page 125

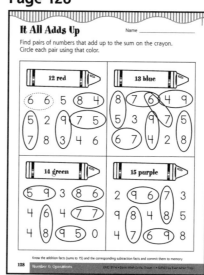

Page 126

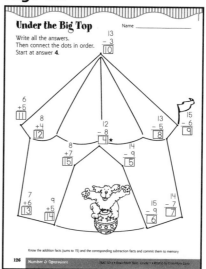

Page 127

1. 6   ⑫   ⑮
2. ⑮   5   5
3. ⑨   7   ⑨
4. ⑮   ⑫   ⑫
5. ⑨   7   ⑭
6. ⑭   7   4

11 peanuts

Page 128

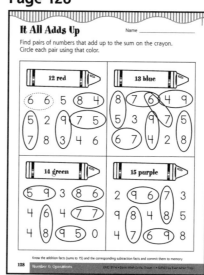

Page 129

1. 15 − 8 = 7
2. 7 + 6 = 13
3. 16 − 9 = 7
4. 7 + 7 = 14
5. Answers will vary, but should represent the picture.

EMC 3014 • Basic Math Skills, Grade 1 • ©2003 by Evan-Moor Corp.

Page 130

1. B 5. D
2. C 6. B
3. A 7. C
4. D 8. B

Page 131

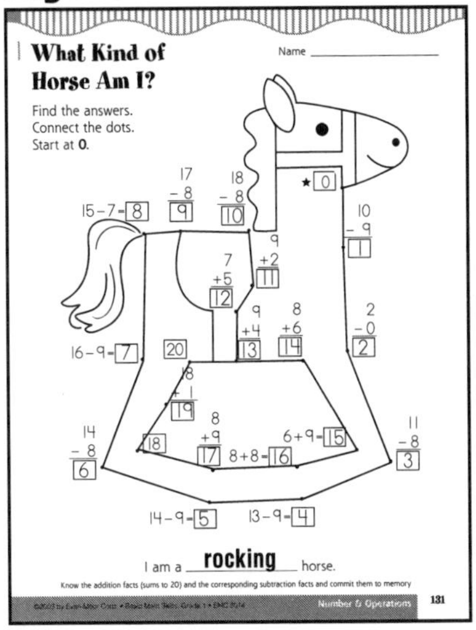

Page 132

6 13 10 15 11 10 16 9 14 8 6 13 15 11 7 15 12 11
a s k u n k w i t h a s u n b u r n

Page 133

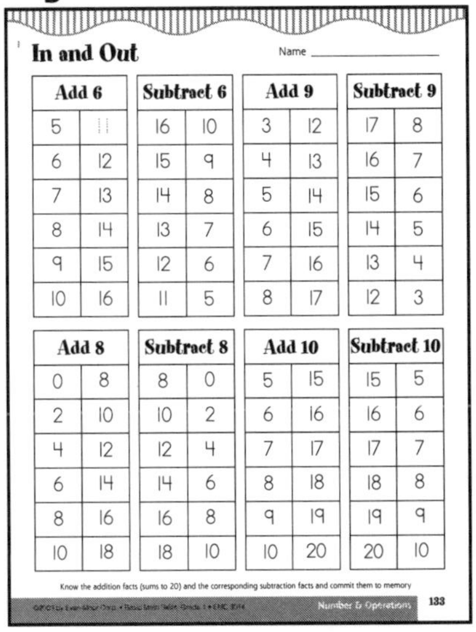

Add 6		Subtract 6		Add 9		Subtract 9	
5	11	16	10	3	12	17	8
6	12	15	9	4	13	16	7
7	13	14	8	5	14	15	6
8	14	13	7	6	15	14	5
9	15	12	6	7	16	13	4
10	16	11	5	8	17	12	3

Add 8		Subtract 8		Add 10		Subtract 10	
0	8	8	0	5	15	15	5
2	10	10	2	6	16	16	6
4	12	12	4	7	17	17	7
6	14	14	6	8	18	18	8
8	16	16	8	9	19	19	9
10	18	18	10	10	20	20	10

Page 134

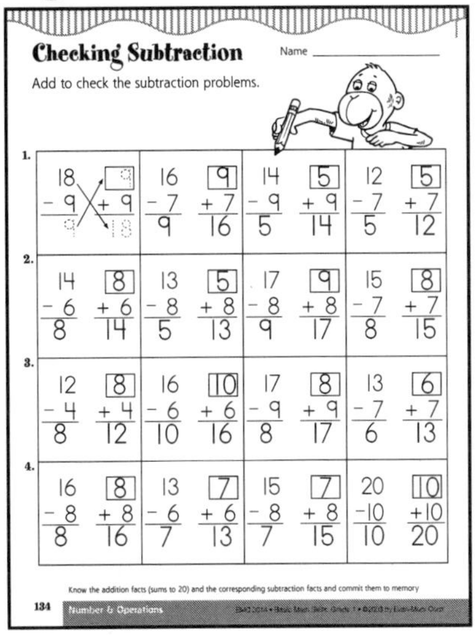

1.	18 − 9 = 9; 9 + 9 = 18	16 − 7 = 9; 9 + 7 = 16	14 − 9 = 5; 5 + 9 = 14	12 − 7 = 5; 5 + 7 = 12
2.	14 − 6 = 8; 8 + 6 = 14	13 − 8 = 5; 5 + 8 = 13	17 − 8 = 9; 9 + 8 = 17	15 − 7 = 8; 8 + 7 = 15
3.	12 − 4 = 8; 8 + 4 = 12	16 − 6 = 10; 10 + 6 = 16	17 − 9 = 8; 8 + 9 = 17	13 − 7 = 6; 6 + 7 = 13
4.	16 − 8 = 8; 8 + 8 = 16	13 − 6 = 7; 7 + 6 = 13	15 − 8 = 7; 7 + 8 = 15	20 − 10 = 10; 10 + 10 = 20

Page 135

1. 9 frogs subtract
2. 18 feet add
3. 8 flies subtract
4. 13 frogs add
5. Word problems will vary, but should reflect the picture.

Page 136

1. C 5. D
2. B 6. C
3. D 7. D
4. B 8. D

Page 137

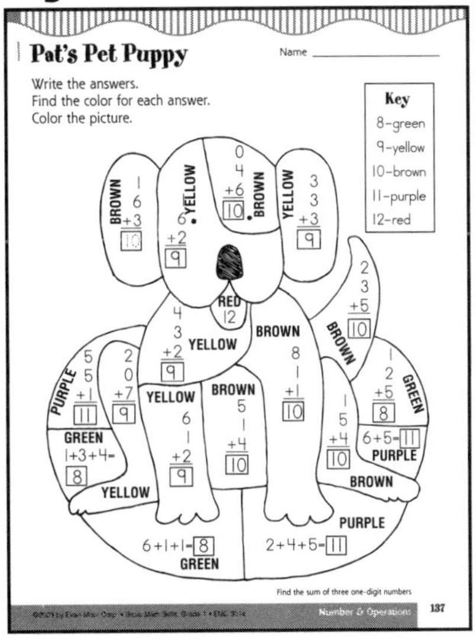

Page 138

1. 10 8 4 6 7
 s n a i l
2. 11 12 9 11 7 5
 t u r t l e

Page 139
1. 2 + 4 + 4 = 10
2. 4 + 0 + 6 = 10
3. 10 + 4 = 14
4. 10 + 2 = 12
5. 10 + 3 = 13
6. 6 + 9 = 15
7. 4 + 8 = 12
8. 8 + 2 = 10

Page 140
1. 9 6 6 7 10 12
2. 12 12 10 11 11 9
3. 13 11 10 12 14 10
4. 14 15 8 7 9 7
5. 14 9 10 11 11 13

Page 141
1. 12 campers
2. 14 leaves
3. 15 fish
4. 14 birds
5. Word problems will vary, but should reflect the picture.

Page 142
1. D   5. D
2. D   6. B
3. B   7. A
4. C   8. D

Page 143
48 38 38 49 53 22 48
r   o   o   s   t   e   r

15 53 65 48 24 22 98
a   t   u   r   k   e   y

Page 144

Page 145
1. 74 88 12 89 27–color 89
2. 22 36 78 55–color 78
3. 48 45 98 14 31–color 98
4. 43 39 70–color 70

Page 146
1. 53 85 ⑮ 88 ⑮
2. 52 ㊻ 86 59 ㊻
3. ㊾ 47 44 ㊾ 88

Page 147
1. 24 – 12 = 12
2. 13 + 16 = 29
3. 36 – 25 = 11
4. 35 + 21 = 56
5. Answers will vary, but should reflect the picture.

Page 148
1. D   5. A
2. B   6. C
3. C   7. C
4. B   8. B

Page 150
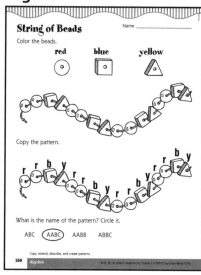

Page 151

EMC 3014 • Basic Math Skills, Grade 1 • ©2003 by Evan-Moor Corp

Page 152

1. <show circle, triangle circled> ABABABAB

2. <show circle, circle, square circled> AABAABAAB

3. <show triangle, rectangle, circle circled> ABCABCABC

4. <show cat, dog, dog, dog circled> ABBBABBB

5. <show daisy, tulip, tulip circled> ABBABBABB

Drawings should show an ABCABC pattern.

Page 153

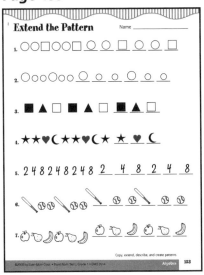

Page 154

Answers will vary, but should meet the criteria of each challenge.

Page 155

1. C	5. A
2. B	6. C
3. A	7. C
4. B	8. D

Page 156

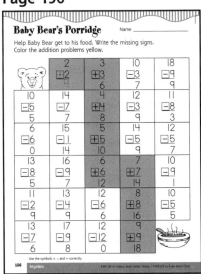

Page 157

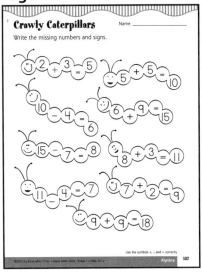

Page 158

1. $6 + 6 = 12$

2. $9 - 3 = 6$

3. $10 + 8 = 18$

4. $15 - 6 = 9$

5. $5 + 2 = 7$

6. $13 - 5 = 8$

Page 159

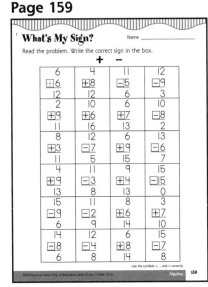

Page 160

1. $11 - 6 = 5$ or $11 - 5 = 6$

2. $4 + 3 = 7$ or $3 + 4 = 7$

3. $4 + 9 = 13$ or $9 + 4 = 13$

4. $15 - 8 = 7$ or $15 - 7 = 8$

5. $8 + 9 = 17$ or $9 + 8 = 17$

6. $13 - 6 = 7$ or $13 - 7 = 6$

Page 161

1. C	5. A
2. B	6. D
3. C	7. C
4. B	8. B

Page 162

Answers will vary.

Page 163

4 + 7 = 11
6 + 7 = 13
6 + 8 = 14
5 + 9 = 14
7 + 10 = 17

Page 164

1. 8¢ + 2¢ = 10¢ (box with 2 pennies)
2. 9¢ + 7¢ = 16¢ (box with 7 pennies)
3. 8¢ + 6¢ = 14¢ (box with 6 pennies)
4. 9¢ + 3¢ = 12¢ (box with 3 pennies)
5. 8¢ + 5¢ = 13¢
6. 9¢ + 4¢ = 13¢
7. 5¢ + 10¢ = 15¢
8. 4¢ + 7¢ = 11¢
9. 10¢ + 10¢ = 20¢
10. 7¢ + 7¢ = 14¢
11. 8¢ + 8¢ = 16¢
12. 5¢ + 5¢ = 10¢

Page 165

1. 4 + 9 = 13
2. 10 − 6 = 4
3. 12 − 8 = 4
4. 5 + 6 = 11

Page 166

Answers will vary, but should reflect the directions.

Page 167

1. C   5. A
2. D   6. D
3. B   7. A
4. C   8. B

Page 169

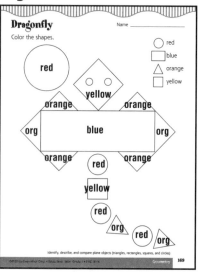

Page 170

to get to the other side

Page 171

1. square   4 sides   4 corners
2. circle   0 sides   0 corners
3. triangle   3 sides   3 corners
4. rectangle   4 sides   4 corners
5. triangle   3 sides   3 corners
6. square   4 sides   4 corners

Page 172

1. picture of a rectangle, parallelogram, or trapezoid
2. picture of a triangle
3. picture of a square or parallelogram
4. picture of a circle
5. They both have 4 sides and 4 corners.
6. A square has sides that are the same length.
   A rectangle doesn't.

Page 173

Pictures will vary, but should include all four kinds of shapes.

Page 174

1. C   5. C
2. B   6. D
3. D   7. C
4. A   8. A

Page 175

EMC 3014 • Basic Math Skills, Grade 1 • ©2003 by Evan-Moor Corp

Page 176

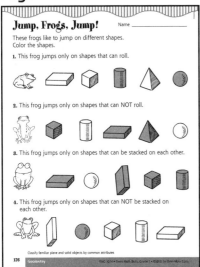

Page 177

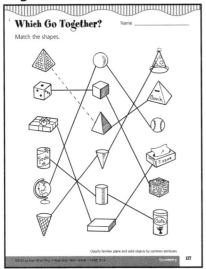

Page 178

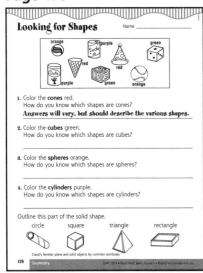

Page 179

Answers will vary.

Page 180

1. D   5. C
2. A   6. D
3. A   7. B
4. D   8. C

Page 181

Page 182

1. sheep/lamb
2. bird/duck
3. pig
4. rabbit/bunny
5. cow
6. horse

Page 183

1. paw print
2. bone
3. collar
4. dog

Page 184

1. school–red
2. flag–red, white, and blue
3. tree–green and brown
4. tetherball–yellow and black
5. a child should be drawn in the sandbox

Page 185

Answers will vary.

Page 186

1. B   5. C
2. D   6. B
3. A   7. C
4. C   8. D

Page 187

Answers will vary, but should reflect the order of the clowns.

Page 188

Answers will vary, but should reflect the placement of the flowers.

Page 189

Answers will vary, but should reflect the placement of the shapes.

Page 190

Answers will vary, but should reflect the placement of the pictures.

Page 191

Answers will vary.

Page 192

1. A   5. A
2. C   6. C
3. A   7. C
4. D   8. C

Page 193

1. no   4. no   7. no
2. yes   5. yes   8. yes
3. yes   6. no   9. no

Page 194

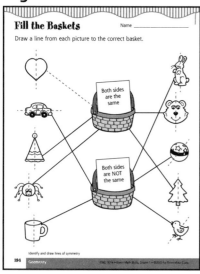

Page 195

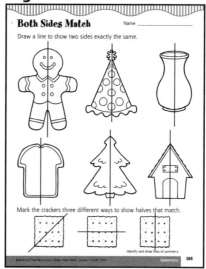

Page 196

Page 197

Answers will vary.

Page 198

1. C   5. D
2. D   6. B
3. C   7. C
4. A   8. D

Page 200

dog	duck	cat	zebra	mouse	sheep
4	2	3	6	1	5

Drawings will vary, but should be accurate.

Page 201

1. giraffe—6 monkeys tall
2. snake—6 monkeys long
3. elephant—5 monkeys wide

EMC 3014 • *Basic Math Skills, Grade 1* • ©2003 by Evan-Moor Corp.

Page 202

doghouse—4 bones
food bowl—2 bones
newspaper—3 bones
dog—6 bones
leash—8 bones

Page 203

1. 2 paper clips
2. 4 paper clips
3. 1 paper clip
4. 3 paper clips
5. 5 paper clips
6. 1 paper clip
7. Answers will vary.

Page 204

Answers will vary.

Page 205

1. D   5. D
2. C   6. B
3. A   7. C
4. C   8. B

Page 206

Answers will vary.

Page 207

Answers will vary.

Page 208

hammer   3 inches
screwdriver 4 inches
wrench   2 inches
saw   6 inches

Page 209

hot dog 6 centimeters   carrot 7 centimeters
peanut 2 centimeters   pretzel 5 centimeters
cookie 3 centimeters   gum 4 centimeters

Page 210

1. 4 − 2 = 2
2. 11 − 4 = 7
3. 14 − 9 = 5
4. 6 − 3 = 3

Page 211

1. A   5. B
2. D   6. D
3. B   7. C
4. D   8. B

Page 212

1. circle bear, **X** monkey
2. circle kangaroo, **X** rabbit
3. circle duck, **X** mouse
4. circle panda, **X** cat

Page 213

1. crocodile
2. rhino
3. elephant
4. lion
5. turkey
6. gorilla

Page 214

1. cup   6. cup
2. cup   7. cup
3. spoon   8. spoon
4. cup   9. cup
5. spoon

Page 215

1. 8 blocks   2. 9 blocks
3. 15 blocks   4. 3 blocks

Page 216

1. bath tub
2. tea kettle
3. bucket
4. jug of juice
5. cup
6. aquarium

Page 217

1. A   5. D
2. D   6. C
3. D   7. C
4. A   8. A

Page 218

Page 219

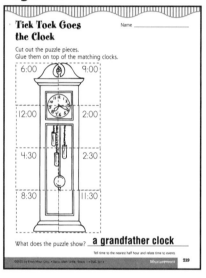

Page 220

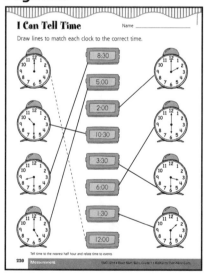

Page 221

1. 4:00
2. 1:30
3. 3:30
4. 8:30
5. 5:00
6. 11:00
7. 2:30
8. 12:00
9. 9:30

Page 222
Answers will vary.

Page 223

1. D
2. B
3. D
4. C
5. D
6. D
7. C
8. A

Page 225

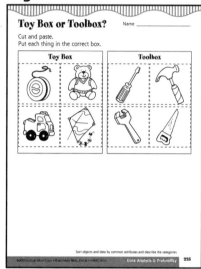

Page 226
Answers will vary, but should be logical.

Page 227

Page 228

1. umbrella; they are all things to wear
2. banana; you can sit on all of them
3. plate; they are all things to eat
4. stapler; you can write with all of them

Page 229

Answers will vary, but should be logical.

Page 230

1. C   5. B
2. B   6. D
3. C   7. C
4. A   8. B

Page 231

1. October
2. September
3. 9 teeth in all
The graph should show three labeled teeth for the month of December.

Page 232

1. vanilla, chocolate, strawberry
2. vanilla—8   strawberry—3   chocolate—10
3. Answers will vary.

Page 233

1. football, baseball, soccer, basketball
2. soccer
3. basketball
4. 15
5. Answers will vary.

Page 234

1. dog
2. snake
3. mouse, hamster
4. Answers will vary.

Page 235

Answers will vary.

Page 236

1. A   5. C
2. C   6. B
3. D   7. C
4. C   8. C

Page 237

Answers will vary.

Page 238

Answers will vary.

Page 239

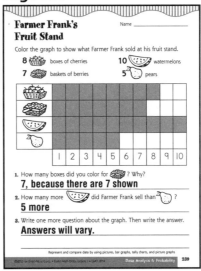

Page 240

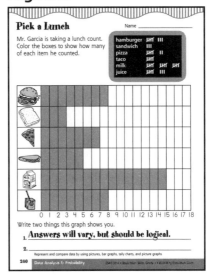

Page 241

Answers will vary.

Page 242

1. C   5. C
2. C   6. A
3. B   7. C
4. A   8. B

Page 244—Timed Tests
Test 1
1 4 5 6 6 6 6 5

5 3 5 2 5 6 6 0

4 6 3 1 2 4 4 3

Test 2
4 6 5 4 2 6 1 5

5 6 6 5 4 1 6 6

3 5 3 4 3 5 2 3

Page 245
Test 3
1 1 1 0 4 3 3 1

4 3 1 0 2 5 1 4

2 2 2 2 0 0 0 3

Test 4
4 4 0 1 3 2 0 5

1 3 3 4 0 0 1 1

5 2 0 2 2 2 0 1

Page 246
Test 5
4 5 0 6 1 0 6 4

3 2 5 2 3 5 1 1

4 4 6 3 1 0 1 6

Test 6
5 2 6 6 2 1 0 4

0 5 3 3 2 6 1 5

4 0 0 4 1 5 1 6

Page 247
Test 7
7 7 10 9 7 10 7 6

10 6 9 9 9 6 8 10

8 7 10 9 9 10 10 9

Test 8
6 7 7 10 7 10 8 7

8 10 10 8 9 9 9 10

9 8 10 7 10 10 9 9

Page 248
Test 9
6 3 3 2 7 0 9 0

0 1 3 2 9 6 10 2

6 1 1 6 5 7 8 7

Test 10
4 8 4 9 1 4 5 5

5 2 3 3 4 5 1 0

6 0 6 1 2 4 1 6

Page 249
Test 11
9 7 10 2 7 6 2 4

4 9 10 5 6 8 5 1

8 7 8 4 0 8 9 6

Test 12
5 7 8 0 7 10 6 10

8 3 2 10 10 1 6 9

10 7 3 10 6 9 7 4

Page 250
Test 13
11 13 10 12 12 13 10 10

12 10 10 12 11 11 10 13

11 10 11 11 10 13 12 12

Test 14
10 11 12 11 13 10 12 13

10 11 13 13 10 11 11 13

13 12 13 10 11 12 10 12

EMC 3014 • Basic Math Skills, Grade 1 • ©2003 by Evan-Moor Cor

Page 251
Test 15
9 6 3 4 7 6 9 0
3 8 5 2 10 7 5 5
1 4 4 8 8 7 2 7

Test 16
10 9 6 6 9 3 4 7
5 9 0 5 7 2 7 8
6 7 8 3 5 4 3 10

Page 252
Test 17
13 9 10 6 13 3 13 4
7 13 11 10 12 7 9 0
11 12 10 8 10 6 13 13

Test 18
1 4 11 4 11 8 12 10
13 12 8 12 5 13 7 5
5 3 11 6 3 2 11 12

Page 253
Test 19
11 13 10 13 13 14 15 14
10 12 10 11 11 15 10 15
10 12 11 14 12 11 14 12

Test 20
13 10 12 15 10 11 11 11
11 10 15 12 12 13 13 15
14 11 12 12 13 11 14 13

Page 254
Test 21
1 9 9 4 2 6 7 3
9 6 4 8 3 5 8 3
5 9 5 5 6 8 8 8

Test 22
7 10 0 9 6 0 14 7
2 8 4 7 4 0 5 7
8 5 3 4 5 9 6 5

Page 255
Test 23
10 10 2 12 12 6 4 13
15 12 9 7 15 2 4 13
12 9 1 15 14 6 9 14

Test 24
12 13 6 3 13 5 13 5
14 6 15 5 14 8 13 7
6 4 14 14 6 8 11 8

Page 256
Test 25
15 11 12 17 13 16 11 13
12 12 14 12 11 11 12 13
11 15 16 11 15 17 13 14

Test 26
12 13 14 14 18 17 13 11
17 15 11 12 11 16 11 15
14 11 16 15 17 12 13 18

Page 257
Test 27
9 7 7 9 8 9 8 2
5 3 5 7 9 4 9 8
6 0 9 9 16 4 9 7

Test 28
10 6 5 8 5 5 4 7
7 9 6 9 9 8 6 4
0 3 9 10 8 7 8 6

Page 258
Test 29

2 13 16 5 14 13 3 8

11 6 7 15 7 12 3 14

16 8 7 14 12 13 5 6

Test 30

7 9 11 15 0 9 14 9

16 8 9 17 11 8 11 14

5 8 8 15 13 4 9 8

EMC 3014 • Basic Math Skills, Grade 1 • ©2003 by Evan-Moor Corp